A POET'S
NOTEBOOK

BLOOMSBURY READER

Discover books by Edith Sitwell published by
Bloomsbury Reader at
www.bloomsbury.com/EdithSitwell

A POET'S NOTEBOOK

EDITH SITWELL

BLOOMSBURY READER

LONDON · NEW DELHI · NEW YORK · SYDNEY

This edition published in 2013 by Bloomsbury Reader

Bloomsbury Reader is a division of Bloomsbury Publishing Plc,

50 Bedford Square, London WC1B 3DP

ISBN: 978 1 4482 0026 9
eISBN: 978 1 4482 0158 7

Contents

Foreword

The aphorisms on Poetry, or applicable to Poetry, with which this book begins were noted down by me, originally, for my private use. All—or nearly all—poets have made examinations into the necessities of Poetry, and I, for one, would rather read by the light of the sun than by lamplight.

In these notes we see Poetry and her necessities as they are seen by the eyes of the poet. These aphorisms throw a light, for me at least, on questions concerning Poetry. I hope they will do this for the readers. Some notes throw lights that are profound, others are like the happy little bee-winged lights of summer, staying for a moment on a flower—they come there purely for pleasure.

Among the most profound lights thrown on the necessities of our time is the aphorism of Baudelaire's on 'the animal of genius', page 4.

There are many aphorisms about Simplicity, firstly because the search for the quintessence, the fusion of elements into a single current—the current that comes from the central core—is one of the principal necessities of Poetry to-day,—secondly because it is believed, by some, that simplicity is shown by debility and a feebleminded lack of muscle.—The right kind of simplicity is the result of 'the hero's immovable core', and is a matter of grandeur and of strength, of perfect balance, of a heroic nakedness, of 'the raw elegance of the Lion'. A return to the savagery of the senses—a voice that speaks 'somewhat above a mortal mouth'—and a grandeur of simplicity—these are among the principal necessities of Poetry at this time. Therefore Baudelaire's saying about the animal of genius, and Leonardo's notes about the olfactory and optic nerves of the lion, have a huge import.

The problems of the various arts touch each other. There are therefore, in this book, many aphorisms which dealt, originally, with music and with painting. They apply, equally, to Poetry.

Some people may cavil at the arrangement of the book. The notes are not arranged chronologically. But the reason for this is, I think, obvious. The shorter notes follow the aphorisms, excepting in the case of a note on the Earliest English Poetry, which belongs, by its nature, to the notes on Chaucer and the notes on early poets which follow those on Chaucer.

Again, it may be asked why I have not included more notes from Wordsworth's, Coleridge's, and Shelley's writings on Poetry. The answer is, that this is my *Notebook*, and that one would not collect *notes* from these writers, excepting in cases where one wishes to underline a remark in its relation to other aphorisms.

I hope that the meanings of the aphorisms, and their relationship to each other, will not be found obscure. For me they are not, and I trust they will not be for others. One can but give what one believes to be the truth. In the words of Whitman, that basely slandered man who was one of the greatest of all poets, that inspired and great soul who has been seen through the dirty eyes of little, mean, and meagre souls—'Whatever satisfies the soul is truth'.

These truths satisfy mine.

EDITH SITWELL

I

On the Poet's Nature

'The sun shone on all statues, but only the statue of Memnon gave forth a sound'.—SCHOPENHAUER ('On the Senses'), *The World as Will and Idea*. Trans. R. B. Haldane and J. Kemp.

'We naturalize ourselves to the employment of eternity.'—BENJAMIN WHICHCOTE, *Aphorisms*.

'His step is the migration of peoples, a migration greater than all ancient invasions'.—ARTHUR RIMBAUD ('Genius'), *Les Illuminations*. Trans. Helen Rootham.

'… countries, and things of which countries are made, elements, planet itself, laws of planets and of men, have passed through this man as bread into his body, and become no longer bread, but body'.—EMERSON ('Plato, or the Philosopher'), *Representative Men*.

' "What", it will be Question'd, "when the Sun rises, do you not see a round disk of fire somewhat like a guinea?" "Oh no,

no, I see an Innumerable Company of the Heavenly Host cry-
ing Holy, Holy, Holy, is the Lord God Almighty." I question not
my Corporeal or Vegetative Eye any more than I would Ques-
tion a Window concerning a Sight. I look thro' it & not with
it'.—BLAKE, *Vision of the Last Judgment*.

The Experience of the Poet during Creation

'… passing from passion to reason, from thanksgiving to ador-
ing, from sense to spirit, from considering ourselves to an union
with God.'—JEREMY TAYLOR, *Holy Living*.

'… this prodigious overflowing of all barriers of phenomenal-
ity must necessarily evoke an incomparable ecstasy in the inspired
musician. … There is but one state that can surpass the musi-
cian's, the state of the Saint; and that, especially because it is
enduring, and incapable of being clouded, whilst the ecstatic
clairvoyance of a musician alternates with an ever-recurring
state of individual consciousness'—WAGNER, *Beethoven*. Trans. E.
Dannreuther.

What is true of the musician is also true of the poet.—E. S.

II

Notes on the Nature of Poetry

1. On Poetry of the Greatest Kind The Fountain-head

'O eternal Truth! and true Charity! and dear Eternity!'.—St. Augustine, *Confessions*.

"… the theme of the Gospel … proclaims Eternity as an event'.—Barth, *The Epistle to the Romans*.

Is not this true of the greatest poetry?—E. S.

'The head Sublime, the heart Pathos, the genitals Beauty, the hands and feet Proportion.'—Blake, *The Marriage of Heaven and Hell*.

'Caedmon … having gone out to the stable of the beasts of burden, the care of which was entrusted to him on that night, and there, at the proper time, having resigned his limbs to sleep, a certain one stood by him in a dream, and said, "Caedmon. … Sing the beginning of created things." '—Bede. Trans. Gidley.

May not the following four aphorisms on Music be applied equally to Poetry of the greatest kind?—E. S.

'Music, as Schopenhauer has made clear to us, is not a representation of the world, but an immediate voice of the world.'—ARTHUR SYMONS, *Studies in Seven Arts*.

'Schopenhauer … recognises in music itself an Idea of the world, wherein the world immediately exhibits its essential nature.'—WAGNER *Beethoven*. Trans. E. Dannreuther.

In Schopenhauer's own words, 'Music never expresses phenomena, but solely the inner being, the essence of phenomena'.—('Metaphysics of Music') *The World as Will and Idea*, quoted as an epilogue in Wagner's *Beethoven*. Trans. E. Dannreuther.

'Music … expresses the inner being, the essence of phenomena, the Will itself, and represents accordingly the metaphysics of all that is physical in the world, the thing *per se*, which lies beyond all appearance.'—*Ibid*.

'The poetic idea which disengages itself from the movement, in the lines, would seem to postulate the existence of a vast being, immense, complicated but of harmonious proportion—an animal full of genius, suffering and sighing all sighs and all human ambitions.'—BAUDELAIRE, *Fusées*.

'… Poetry, prophecy, and the high insight, are from a wisdom of which man is not master … the gods never philosophise.'—EMERSON ('Plato, or the Philosopher'), *Representative Men*.

'Music … would seem to reveal the most secret sense of scene, action, event, environment.'—WAGNER, *Beethoven*. Trans. E. Dannreuther.

Is not this also true of Poetry?—E. S.

'As Christianity arose from under the civilisation of Rome, so from the Chaos of modern civilisation music burst forth. Both affirm: "Our kingdom is not of this world". That is to say, "We come from within, you from without. We spring from the essential nature of things, you from its semblance."'—WAGNER *Beethoven*. Trans. E. Dannreuther.

Poetry of the greatest kind springs from the essential nature of things, not from its semblance. But poetry has its phenomena in nature, its outward and revelatory being. Poetry is also the visible world, with its images of wonder.—E. S.

Cézanne declared, 'I have not tried to produce Nature; I have represented it.'—Quoted in MARTIN ARMSTRONG'S *The Major Pleasures of Life*.

This great painter must be held to be right, according to the necessities of the art of which he was a practitioner. But in Poetry the exact opposite is right. To represent Nature, in Poetry, would mean, not that Nature is heard or seen through a temperament, but that Nature was un-assimilated by the poet, had not 'passed into this man as bread into his body'. (See page 1.)—E. S.

The greatest poet has a 'strong solving sense to reconcile his poetry with the appearances of the world'.—EMERSON ('Plato, or the Philosopher'), *Representative Men*.

'Music blots out an entire civilisation as sunshine does lamplight.'—WAGNER, *Beethoven*. Trans. E. Dannreuther.

This is true of the greatest poetry in a certain kind. It is true of Shakespeare's Comedies. In another kind, poetry is a sun whose light does not blot out a civilisation, but fuses it into a single being. This is true of certain of Shakespeare's characters.—E. S.

'The Greeks said that Alexander went as far as Chaos; Goethe went, only the other day, as far; and one step farther he hazarded, and brought himself straight back'.—EMERSON ('Goethe, or the Writer'), *Representative Men*.

'He' (Goethe) 'had a power to unite the detached atoms again by their own law'.—*Ibid*.

'He' (Plato), 'from the sunlike centrality and reach of his vision, had a faith without cloud'.—EMERSON ('Plato, or the Philosopher'), *Representative Men*.

'Can no father beget or mother conceive a man-child so entire and so elastic that whatever … syllable he speaks, it shall be melodious to all creatures, and none shall be an exception to the universal and affectionate "Yes" of the earth?'—WHITMAN, *Notebooks*.

'If I speak with the tongues of men and of angels, but have not love, I am become sounding brass, or a clanging cymbal. And if I have the gift of prophecy, and know all mysteries and all knowledge; and if I have all faith, so as to remove mountains, but have not love, I am nothing.'—St. Paul, I Corinthians xiii.

'We have done nothing … if we have not purified the will in the order of charity.'—St. John of the Cross, *Ascent of Mount Carmel*.

'Thought without affection makes a distinction between Love and Wisdom as it does between body and spirit.'—BLAKE (annotations to Swedenborg's *Wisdom of Angels Concerning Divine Love and Divine Wisdom*), *Marginalia*.

'His' (the greatest poet's) 'brain is the ultimate brain. He is no arguer, he is judgment. He judges not as the judge judges, but as the sun falling around a helpless, thing. As he sees the farthest, he has the most faith. His thoughts are the hymns of the praise of things … he sees eternity in men and women,—he does not see men and women as dreams or dots. … Now he has passed that way, see after him! there is not left any vestige of despair or misanthropy or cunning or exclusiveness, or the ignominy of a nativity or colour, or delusion of hell or the necessity of hell; and no man thenceforward shall be degraded for ignorance or weakness or sin.'—WHITMAN, Preface to *Leaves of Grass*.

(It may be held that the above should have been placed under the heading of 'The Greatest Poet', but to my feeling it belongs where I have placed it.—E. S.)

'See the mysteries which lie hid in that miracle of Our Lord' (the changing of Water into Wine). (The) 'Scriptures were the water. He made the water wine when He opened unto them the meaning of these things, and expounded the Scriptures; for thus that came to have a taste which before had none, and that inebriated which did not inebriate before.'—ST. AUGUSTINE, quoted in St. Thomas: *Catena Aurea*.

The poets, among the sons of God, must keep this miracle, humbly, before their minds. They must open the meaning of the visual world, which, for them, is among the Scriptures.—E. S.

'Now was I come up in spirit through the flaming sword into the Paradise of God. All things were new: and all the Creation gave another smell unto me than before.'—GEORGE FOX, *Journal*.

'Poetry is the identity of all other knowledges, the blossom and fragrance of all human knowledge, human thoughts,

7

human passions, emotions, language.'—COLERIDGE, *Biographia Literaria*.

'All truths lie waiting in all things. … For their birth you need not the obstetric forceps of the surgeon. They unfold themselves more fragrant than … roses from living buds, whenever you fetch the spring sunshine moistened with summer rain. But it must be in yourself. … It shall be love.'—WHITMAN, *Notebooks*.

'Poetry is the Honey of all Flowers, the Quintessence of all Sciences, the Marrow of Art and the very Phrase of Angels.'— THOMAS NASHE.

(I noted this, but cannot now trace the original quotation, which has been with me for many years. It is quoted by Mr. de la Mare, in *Come Hither.*—E. S.)

'Bless Jesus Christ with the Rose and his people, which is a nation of living sweetness.'—SMART, *Rejoice with the Lamb*.

'Bless God with every feather from the Wren in the sedge to the Cherubs and their mates.'—*Ibid*.

'I would believe only in a God that knew how to dance.'— NIETZSCHE, *Thus Spake Zarathustra*.

'Rowland, Rowland, get up and see the sun dance.'—A countrywoman of Hockley, early one Easter morning, to her husband. Told in MRS. WRIGHT'S *Rustic Speech and Folklore*.

This is like reading *As You Like It* for the first time.—E. S.

'All the pain of existence is shattered against the immense delight of playing … with the power of shaping the incomprehensible. … Brahma, the Creator of worlds, laughs as he perceives the illusion about himself; innocence regained plays lightly with the sting of expiated guilt, conscience set free banters itself with the torments it has undergone.'—WAGNER, *Beethoven*. Trans. E. Dannreuther.

'Perfection of a thing is threefold: first, according to the constitution of its own being; secondly, in respect of any accidents being added as necessary for its perfect operation; thirdly, perfection consists in the attaining to something else as the end. ... This triple perfection belongs to no creature by its own essence; it belongs to God only, in Whom alone essence is existence.'— AQUINAS, *Summa Theologica*.

The perfection of the spiritual life, as given here, is of the same order as the perfection of a poem.—E. S.

2. Of the Great Poems from the Depths

'What prodigies may we not conceive of ...' (from) "those primitive longæval and antediluvian man-tigers, who first taught science to the world.'—MARTIN SCRIBLERUS, *On the Origin of Sciences*.

'... Satan's Mathematic Holiness, Length, Bredth, & Highth'.— BLAKE, *Milton*, Book the Second.

'As I was walking among the fires of Hell, delighted with the enjoyments of Genius, which to Angels look like torment and insanity, I collected some of their Proverbs, thinking that as the sayings used in a nation mark its character, so the Proverbs of Hell show the nature of infernal wisdom.'—BLAKE, *Marriage of Heaven and Hell*.

'... the notion that man has a body distinct from his soul is to be expunged; this I shall do by printing in the infernal method, by corrosives, which in Hell are salutary and medicinal, melting apparent surfaces away, and displaying the infinite which was hid.'—*Ibid.*

'I constantly thought of the saying that when Delacroix paints, it is exactly like a lion devouring a piece of flesh.'—VAN GOGH, *Letters of a Post-Impressionist.* Trans. Anthony M. Ludovici.

Baudelaire, speaking of Delacroix, quotes an acquaintance as saying that his is 'cannibal painting'.—BAUDELAIRE, *L'Art Romantique.*

Millet said: 'In art, it is necessary to put our very skin .'— Quoted in VAN GOGH's *Letters to an Artist.*

(NOTE.—Which are the great poems from the depths? ... Such works, say, as *King Lear, Timon of Athens,* Villon's *Le Grand Testament,* and our traditional *Tom o' Bedlam's Song.*—These I have named are only a few. 'The Tyger' has moved through the depths, but he has also walked in heaven.—E. S.)

3. Of Lyrical Poems and other Poems of a Small, but Perfect, Kind

'... The lark is a mighty angel.'—BLAKE, *Milton,* Book the Second.

'The verse which out of many vocables remakes an entire word, new, unknown to the language, and as if magical, attains this isolation of speech.'—MALLARMÉ, excerpt from a Lecture. Trans. Arthur Symons, in *The Symbolist Movement in French Literature.*

'I say: "A flower!" and out of the oblivion to which my voice consigns every contour, so far as anything save the known calyx, musically arises, idea, and exquisite, the one flower absent from all bouquets.'—*Ibid.*

'To create a little flower is the labour of ages.'—BLAKE, *The Marriage of Heaven and Hell.*

Little, yet perfect. The verses of Austin Dobson, and kindred horrors, are not perfect. They are merely slippery. Certain short poems of Blake, and such a poem as 'He came also stil where his mother was', are among the most wonderful examples of the little, yet perfect kind.—E. S.

'A flower told me her name.'—RIMBAUD, *Les Illuminations.* Trans. Helen Rootham.

The poems of Herrick might be an example of this small, yet perfect kind. They have not the childlike humble ecstasy of the short Blake poems, or of 'He came al so stil'—they are not the flower itself, like those mysterious growths,—but the flower certainly told its secret name to Herrick.—E. S.

'The greatest poet hardly knows pettiness or triviality. If he breathes into anything that was before thought small, it dilates with the grandeur and life of the universe.'—WHITMAN, Preface to *Leaves of Grass.*

'Snow quickly becomes marble in the predestinate hands.'— COCTEAU ('Carte Blanche,'), *Le Rappel à l'Ordre.*

'The artist who has the sentiment of reality must never fear to be lyrical. The objective world retains its power in his work, no matter to what metamorphoses lyricism may have subjected it.'—COCTEAU ('Le Coq et l'Arlequin'), *Le Rappel à l'Ordre.*

11

'To know how cherries and strawberries taste, said he, ask children and birds.'—GOETHE, listening to 'the songs and yodelling of the cheerful Tyrolese': *Conversations of Goethe with Eckermann*. Trans. J. Oxenford.

The above seems to me applicable to some of the lovely folk-songs that are the natural growth of our soil:' The Turtle-Dove,' 'Under the Leves Grene' (an early poem, anonymous, but not actually a folk-song), 'Oh dear, what can the matter be' and hundreds of others. Also to many of the sweet and exquisite nursery rhymes. In these respects I, for one, am both child and bird.—E. S.

4. *Applicable to Modern Poetry*

'The direct trial of him who would be the greatest poet is today. If he does not flood himself with the immediate age as with vast oceanic tides—and if he does not attract his own land body and soul to himself … and if he be not himself the age transfigured—and if to him is not opened the eternity which gives similitude to all periods and locations and processes and animate and inanimate forms, and which is the bond of time …' (the eternity which) 'commits itself to the representation of this wave of an hour, and this one of the sixty beautiful children of the wave—let him merge in the general run and wait his development. …'—WHITMAN, Preface to *Leaves of Grass*.

This is right for the transcendentally great poet who wrote it, but it is not right for every poet, even every great poet. It is certainly never right for the small poet, under any circumstances. On this subject, van Gogh (*Letters of a Post-Impressionist*, trans. Anthony M. Ludovici) said we must 'avoid squandering our modest powers in metaphysical brooding which cannot press chaos into a tumbler; for that is precisely why it is chaos, because it cannot enter into a tumbler of our calibre'. This should be remembered.—E. S.

We must learn 'to cram today with Eternity and not the next day'.—KIERKEGAARD, *Christian Discourses*.

'... poetry sheds no tears "such as Angels weep", but natural and human tears; she can boast of no celestial ichor that distinguishes her vital juices from those of prose; the same human blood circulates through the veins of them both.'—WORDSWORTH, Preface to *Lyrical Ballads* (1800–1805).

This belief has produced, often, wonderful results in the case of the great poet who declared it. But it is profoundly dangerous. Poetry should 'utter somewhat above a mortal mouth', to quote a phrase from Ben Jonson's *Discoveries*.—E. S.

'Art is Science become flesh.'—COCTEAU ('Le Secret Professionnel') *Le Rappel à l'Ordre*.

'Pure draughtsmen are philosophers and the abstractors of the quintessence.'—BAUDELAIRE, *Curiosités Esthétiques*.

Many modern poets may be considered as draughtsmen—in their precision, avoidance of superfluity, vagueness, or romanticism.—E. S.

'Ô Soleil, c'est le temps de la Raison ardente.'

I read somewhere, and now cannot trace, this line by Guillaume Apollinaire. I think that poetry, at this time, lives in the weather of the 'Raison ardente'.—E. S.

'Genius can no more analyse itself than can electricity. Either one possesses it, or one does not possess it. ... Stravinsky canalises a brute force and so uses it that it serves equally the apparatus from the workshop, and the pocket lamp.'—COCTEAU ('Le Coq et l'Arlequin', Appendice 1924), *Le Rappel à l'Ordre*.

'As you see, we are not far from the religious spirit. ... The primordial importance that is granted to lyricism by minds like ours, the most capable, one would have thought, of despising it, obliges us to recognise in it a divine essence.

'This can change the slightest object into an idol, and make it live, for us, in conditions of an astounding silence.'—COCTEAU ('Le Secret Professionel'), *Le Rappel à l'Ordre*.

'The spirit of poetry: the religious spirit outside all precise religion, is doubtless what Paul Claudel depicted perfectly when he told us that Rimbaud was a mystic in the wild state.'—*Ibid.*

Among the characteristics of modern poetry at its best, as of modern painting at its best, is the extraordinary and almost terrifying *identity* of that idol, the subject,—an identity which is due, in part, to simplicity, to the stripping away of all superfluities (see the section on Simplicity, page 34), and the extraordinary, almost terrifying silence by which the idol is surrounded.—E. S.

To speak of certain modern painters, for in these qualities the poets resemble the painters, in a recent essay on Tchelitchew, in the quarterly *View* (May 1942), Mr. Lincoln Kirstein wrote, 'In his' (Tchelitchew's) 'later paintings, as in Seurat, objects indicated exist isolated in their own air. ... Each has its own essential temporal and spatial independence.'

In the same number of this quarterly, Nicholas Calas, writing of Yves Tanguy, said, 'The appalling silence of Tanguy's pictures creates a longing for sound. ... The changes of temperature are rhythmical.' He adds, 'The solitude of Tanguy is oceanic'.

In poetry, the subject, itself a life of sound, is surrounded by this silence.—In certain poems, it might be said that the changes of rhythm, of speed, are like changes in temperature.—E. S.

'The depths are fathomless, and therefore calm. The innocence and nakedness are resumed.'—WHITMAN, Preface to *Leaves of Grass*.

'More enigmas are contained in the shadow of a man walking in the light of the sun, than in all religions, past, present, or future.'—CHIRICO, writing in the quarterly *Minotaure*.

This is an exaggeration. To have said 'as many' would have been truer. But it is from enigmas such as these that the modern poet waits to hear a voice, the voice that spoke in the groves of Dodona, the voice of the Sphinx.—E. S.

'Here you will see no trace of any monument or superstition. Morality and language are reduced to their simplest expression. ... New Erinnyes haunt the cottage which is my country and the home of my desires—Death without tears our active handmaid, hopeless Love, and a pretty little crime whining in the street.'—RIMBAUD ('A Town'), *Illuminations*. Trans. Helen Rootham.

'Great is the faith of the flush of knowledge, and of the investigation of the depths of qualities and things. Cleaving and circling here swells the soul of the poet.'—WHITMAN, Preface to *Leaves of Grass*.

'The culte of a ruin hides ... the sound of the shock of intelligence against beauty.'—COCTEAU ('Picasso'), *Le Rappel à l'Ordre*.

15

5. Applicable to Works of a Certain Kind

(NOTE.—There is more music than poetry of this nature. For instance, certain works of Stravinsky's are of this order. In poetry, my verses for William Walton's and my joint work *Façade* are examples of this kind.—E. S.)

Warning: The 'raw elegance of the lion is dangerous'.— COCTEAU, writing of Braque ('Le Coq et l'Arlequin'), *Le Rappel à l'Ordre*.

Villiers de l'Isle Adam wrote of his own work, *Triboulat Bon-homet*, that it was 'an enormous and sombre clowning, the colour of the century'.

All nations, and particularly the English, are slow to understand works of this nature. At first, these works are derided, and their authors insulted; then, twenty years after their first appearance, the point of such works is seen.

It is certain that an empty work which appears to be serious because it is dull will be acclaimed as a masterpiece, while a work of the above order will be at first disdained.—E. S.

Cocteau, writing in 'Le Coq et l'Arlequin' (*Le Rappel à l'Ordre*) of a great work of this nature, the ballet *Parade*, of which he, Picasso, and Satie were the authors, said, 'For the majority of artists a work cannot be beautiful without a plot, involving mysticism, love, or boredom. Brevity, gaiety, sadness without romance are suspect. The hypocritical elegance of the Chinaman, the melancholy of the Little Girl's steamboats, the touching silliness of the Acrobats, all that which has remained a dead letter to the public, would have pleased them, if the Acrobat had been in love with the Little Girl, and had been killed by the jealous

16

Chinaman, who had then been killed, in his turn, by the wife of the Acrobat—or any of the other thirty-six dramatic combinations'.

'… we become drunk with a strong honey, and that honey must sometimes be gathered from the paw of a very young bear.'—Cocteau, writing about Poulenc ('Le Coq et l'Arlequin'), *Le Rappel à l'Ordre*.

Works of this order have, from time to time, this wild and heady sweetness, attached to menace.—E. S.

'It is the poetry of childhood overtaken by a technician.'—Cocteau, writing of Satie's music for *Parade*. *Ibid*.

Works of this order, in poetry, are frequently technical experiments of an extreme difficulty.—E. S.

'Purely arithmetical relations', wrote Schopenhauer—('Metaphysics of Music') *The World as Will and Idea*—'lie at the foundation of both rhythm and melody; in the one case, the relative duration of the notes, in the other case, the relative rapidity of their vibrations. … The rhythmical element is the essential; for it can produce a kind of melody of itself alone … and without the other …'

This is the case with a work such as *Façade*, where in many cases (though not, for instance, in such poems as 'By the Lake', 'Daphne', 'Four in the Morning', or 'Rose and Alice') the rhythmical element has produced the melody.—E. S.

(See 'On Technical Experiments,' page 27.)

The mention of technical experiments brings us to the question of distortion.

Guillaume Apollinaire (*Méditations Esthétiques*) wrote: 'The Fourth Dimension, such as it is, offers itself to the intellect from the plastic point of view, is the immensity of space, eternalising itself in all directions at a determined moment. It is space itself, the dimension of the infinite; it is this which endows objects with plasticity. It gives them, in a word, the proportions they deserve, whereas in Greek Art, for example, a rhythm that is to a certain degree mechanical ceaselessly destroys the proportions.

'Greek Art had a purely human conception of beauty. It took Man as the measure of perfection. The Art of the new painters takes the infinite universe as the ideal, and it is to that ideal that we owe a new measure of perfection which allows the artist to give to the object proportions conformable to the degree of plasticity which he wishes to produce in it. Nietzsche divined the possibilities of such an Art.

' "O Dionysus divine, why dost thou pull mine ears?" Ariadne asks her philosophical lover in one of the celebrated dialogues on the Isle of Naxos. "I find there is something agreeable, something pleasant about thine ears. … Why are they not still longer?" …

'Nietzsche, when he recounts this anecdote, brings to trial, through the lips of Dionysus, Greek Art.'—APOLLINAIRE, *Les Peintres Artistes*.

'Words and thoughts, never before brought together since Babel, clash into a protesting combination, and in the very aspect of the page there is something startling.'—ARTHUR SYMONS, writing on Villiers de l'Isle Adam, in *Baudelaire: a Study*.

I would have substituted 'civilisation' for 'combination'.—E. S.

'Charm needs a profound tact. One must cling to the edge of vacancy. Nearly all graceful artists fall over the edge. Rossini, Tchaikowski, Weber, Gounod, Chabrier … lean over, but do not fall. They have a deep root, and this allows them to lean very far.'—COCTEAU ('Le Coq et l'Arlequin'), *Le Rappel à l'Ordre.*

'Everything which grows with irresistible force is accused of arrivism.'—COCTEAU ('Le Secret Professionel'), *Le Rappel à l'Ordre.*

'You will say to me "No solitude lasts long. You will soon see the school of solitude, or the school of the tightrope." It is possible; but as it is dangerous, it does not attract everybody.

'As for the rest, one of the secrets of the *tour de force* lies in deceiving disciples, if they appear.

'How shall they be deceived?

'Ah, gentlemen, turn over our worlds, our pockets. ... One risks nothing in divulging the professional secret. The means of using it are lacking.'—COCTEAU ('D'un Ordre considéré comme une Anarchie'), *Le Rappel à l'Ordre.*

Alas, Monsieur Cocteau was over-optimistic. *Nothing* will prevent amateurs from imitating, and spoiling the works they imitate. I defy anyone to escape from them. Simplicity itself—the simplicity of the great master, that most uncopyable of all forces, is imitated.—E. S.

III

Notes on Technical Matters

1. On Texture

'It is,' wrote Richard Wagner in his book, on Beethoven, 'a matter of experience that, by the side of the world which presents itself as visible in waking as well as in dreaming, we are conscious of yet another world which manifests itself by sound ... a true world of sound by the side of a world of light, of which it may be said that it bears the same relation to the latter as dreaming to waking.'

It is with this world of sound that many of the notes in this book deal.

Histories of English prosody have occupied themselves mainly with the effect on rhythm of variety and changes of accent, and the effect of alliteration; but, as far as I know, although Mr. Robert Graves has written a highly interesting chapter on Texture itself ('Techniques of Modern Poetry')—as I said in my book on Alexander Pope, the effect of texture upon rhythm and upon speed have not been considered. The truth is, that the texture of a poem has been regarded as merely a matter of fatness or leanness—has been acknowledged only as producing richness, or sweetness, or harshness in the poem; but the fact that texture is largely responsible for rhythm, and for variations in the speed of the poem, have not been acknowledged. The particular part played by the varying uses of consonants, vowels, labials, and sibilants, has been insufficiently considered.—E. S.

With regard to the relationship of consonants and vowels, it might, perhaps, be said that the vowels are the spirit, the consonants and labials the physical identity, with all the variations of harshness, hairiness, coldness, roughness, smoothness, etc.[1] (E. S.), 'the garment of the spirit, "thus distinguished, marked off and announced ... to the outer world," (as) "the animal by the skin, the tree by its bark " '.—WAGNER, 'Opera and Drama', Part II, *Prose Works*. Trans. W. A. Ellis.

'We have called' (Wagner explains in 'The Theatre', *Prose Works*, Part III., trans. W. A. Ellis) 'the consonants, the garments of the vowel, or, more precisely, the physiognomic exterior. ... Just as it hedges the vowel from without, so does it also bound the vowel within ... *i.e.* it determines the specific nature of the latter's manifestment, through the roughness or smoothness of the inward contact therewith ... or, to elaborate the matter further, these enclosing consonants are playing the part of the fleshly covering of the human body, organically ingrown

---

[1] Dante wrote of consonants being 'shaggy' and 'buttered', *pesca et hirsuto*, 'combed and hairy'.

with the interior; we shall thus gain a faithful image of the essence both of consonant and vowel, as well as of the organic relations to one another. Take the vowel for the whole inner organism of man's living body, which prescribes from out itself the shaping of its outward show, as offered to the eye of the beholder.'[2]

Cézanne declared that 'when colour has its richness, form has its plenitude'.[3] This is applicable to the effect that vowels have upon consonants.—E. S.

'Bodies serve light, which would not shine unless it could break against them; similarly it may be said that without rhythm music would not be perceptible.'—WAGNER, *Beethoven*. Trans. E. Dannreuther.

This is the service rendered by the consonants to the spiritual force of the vowels.

Consonants have each, when in contact with the vowel, their own specific gravity, mobility, or want of elasticity, their power of refracting light, their behaviour as magnetic or diagmagnetic.

Consonants shape; they do not affect time as do vowels: roughly speaking the realm of consonants is in Space: the realm of vowels in Time—although vowels, too, have their place, position, depth, and height, they do not give body.

Sibilants slow the line.—E. S.

---

[2] In certain early, or fairly early poetry, and in certain fairly late poetry in which there is an alliterative scheme—such as Dunbar's 'Blind Harry'—consonants have another rôle. See the note on Dunbar.

[3] Cézanne, quoted in *Major Pleasures of Life*, Martin Armstrong.

2. On Technical Perfection

'... the feature in Beethoven's musical productions which is so particularly momentous for the history of art is this: that here, every technical detail, by means of which for clearness' sake the artist places himself in a conventional relation to the external world, is raised to the highest significance of a spontaneous effusion.'—WAGNER, *Beethoven*. Trans. E. Dannreuther.

This should be true of all technique.—E. S.

'Mechanical excellence is the only vehicle of genius.'—BLAKE, *Marginalia:* Reynolds' Discourses.

'Without innate Neatness of Execution, the Sublime cannot exist.'—*Ibid.*

'The fruition of beauty is no chance of hit or miss—it is inevitable as life—it is exact and plumb as gravitation. From the eyesight proceeds another eyesight, and from the hearing proceeds another hearing ... eternally curious of the harmony of things with man. To these respond perfections.'—WHITMAN, Preface to *Leaves of Grass.*

'His' (Plato's) 'strength is like the momentum of a falling planet; and his discretion, the return of its due and perfect curve—so excellent is his Greek love of boundary, and his skill in definition.'—EMERSON ('Plato, or the Philosopher'), *Representative Men.*

This should be true of all technique.—E. S.

'The great and golden rule of Art as well as of Life, is that the more distinct, [and] sharp ... the bounding line, the more perfect the work of art; and the less keen and sharp, the greater is the evidence of weak imitation, plagiarism, and bungling. ... What is it that distinguishes honesty from knavery, but the hard ... line of rectitude and certainty, in the actions and intentions? Leave out this line, and you leave out life itself; all is chaos again, and the line of the Almighty must be drawn out upon it, before man or beast can exist.'—BLAKE, *Descriptive Catalogue*.

This refers to drawing, but is equally applicable to poetry. It should be learned by heart by the woolly imitators of that great poet, Wordsworth.—E. S.

'Energy is the only life, and is from the Body; and Reason is the bound or outward circumference of Energy.'—BLAKE, *Marriage of Heaven and Hell*.

All technical achievement is, as it were, the Etheric Body of the poet.—E. S.

3. On the Essence of Sound

SOCRATES: ... Is there not an essence of colour and sound as of anything else which may be said to be an essence. ... And if anyone could imitate the essence of each thing in letters and syllables, would he not express the nature of each thing?'

SOCRATES: 'That objects should be imitated in letters and syllables and so find expression may appear ridiculous, Hermogenes, but it cannot be avoided.'—('Cratylus') *The Dialogues of Plato*.

'Imitate': should not the word be 'reproduce'? If we *imitate* an essence, it is false.—E. S.

'The angels, from the sound of the voice, know a man's love; from the articulation of the sound, his wisdom; and from the sense of his words, his science.'—SWEDENBORG, quoted by

Emerson ('Swedenborg the Mystic'), *Representative Men.*

'Sounds as well as thoughts have relation both between each other and towards that which they represent, and a perception of the order of those relations has always been found connected with a perception of the order of the relations of thoughts. Hence the language of poets has ever affected a certain uniform and harmonious recurrence of sound, without which it were not poetry, and which is scarcely less indispensable to the communication of its influence, than the words themselves, without reference to that peculiar order. Hence the vanity of translation; it were as wise to cast a violet into a crucible that you might discover the formal principle of its colour and odour, as seek to transfuse from one language into another the creations of a poet. The plant must spring again from its seed, or it will bear no flower—and this is the burthen of the curse of Babel.'—SHELLEY, *A Defence of Poetry.*

This is true of translations in nearly all cases. But there are wonderful exceptions. The translations by Arthur Waley from the Japanese and Chinese are works of a transcendental beauty—the pure essence of beauty itself, as indefinable as the scent of a flower. I know nothing more lovely than these truly miraculous works.—E. S.

'Like the metamorphosis of things into higher forms, is their change into melodies. Over every thing stands its dæmon or soul, and as the form of the thing is reflected by the eye, so the soul of the thing is reflected by a melody. The sea, the mountain-ridge, Niagara, and every flower-bed, pre-exist, or super-exist, in precantations, which sail like odours in the air, and when any man goes by with an ear sufficiently fine, he overhears them, and endeavours to write down the notes, without diluting or depraving them, and herein is the legitimation of criticism in the mind's faith, that the poems are a corrupt version of some text in nature, with which they ought to be made to tally.'—EMERSON ('The Poet'), *Essays*.

'Melody,' said Beethoven,' is the sensual life of poetry. Do not the spiritual contents of a poem become sensual feeling through melody?'—Quoted by G. H. LEWES, *Inner Life of Art*.

4. On Rhythm

Rhythm has been defined as 'melody stripped of its pitch'. This should be remembered.—E. S.

Wagner wrote: 'Rhythm is the mind of dance and the skeleton of tone.' 'Tone is the heart of man through which dance and poetry are brought to mutual understanding.' 'This organic being is clothed upon with the flesh of the world.'—Quoted by ARTHUR SYMONS, *Studies in Seven Arts*.

For the word 'Tone' substitute 'texture', which is to poetry what tone is to music,—and for Wagner's use of the word 'poetry' substitute 'the spirit'.—The flesh of the world is made, for poetry, of the varying and shaping consonants. Vowels are the heart of tone.—E. S. (See Notes on Texture, pages 18 and 19).

'Rhythm is in time what symmetry is in space.'—SCHOPENHAUER, *The World as Will and Idea*. Trans. T. B. Haldane and J. Kemp.

'Time is primarily the form of inner sense.'—SCHOPENHAUER ('Of Knowledge à Priori'), *The World as Will and Idea*.

Rhythm, then, is the form of inner sense when it has attained full consciousness and has become executive. Rhythm is the executive Sense or Soul.—E. S.

'... the Musician, moulding and shaping, stretches his hand, as it were, towards the waking world of phenomena, by the *rhythmical* succession of *time* in his productions, much as the allegorical stream connects with the habitual ideas of the individual, so that the waking consciousness, which is turned towards the external world, is able firmly to retain it.'—WAGNER, *Beethoven*. Trans. E. Dannreuther.

(Rhythm, therefore, is one of the principal translators between dream and reality.—E. S.)

'Thus,' Wagner continues, 'by means of the rhythmical arrangement of tones, the musician touches upon the perceptible plastic world.'

This is also true of the poet.

Rhythm might be described as, in the world of sound, what light is in the visible world. It shapes, and it gives new meaning.—E. S.

'Beethoven contemplates life, and appears to contemplate how he is to play a dance for life itself.'—WAGNER, *Beethoven*.

5. On the Modern Use of Rhythm

'It is a weakness not to comprehend the beauty of a machine. The fault lies in depicting machines instead of taking from them a lesson in rhythm, in stripping away the superfluous.'—COCTEAU ('Carte Blanche'), *Le Rappel à l'Ordre*.

'To describe a dreadnought is no more new than to describe a galley. What is new is that one should feel in the poem the rhythm of a dreadnought, as Racine evokes the pomp of a galley. Onomatopea relegates us to the rank of a parrot—(even that which Marinetti calls 'abstract onomatopea'). A spectacle, a sound, which

27

enters through the eye and the ear, should be subjected, before it reissues by the hand, to profound metamorphoses.'—*Ibid.*

6. On Form

'In each era of poetry, outward structure must inevitably undergo a change. In the Augustan age, the outward structure of poetry was the result of logic alone, while variations of speed, the feeling of heat and of cold, the variations of the different depths and heights, were produced by means of texture and were the result of sensibility and of instinct in this matter. Poetry was therefore, in that age, as far as outward structure was concerned, the sister of architecture. With the Romantics and their more poignant vowel-sense, resulting in a different kind of melodic line, poetry became the sister of music. Now she appears like the sister of horticulture—each poem growing according to the laws of its own nature, but in a line which is more often the irregular though entirely natural shape of a tree,—bearing leaves, bearing fruit,—than a sharp melodic line, springing like a fountain.'—E. S., *Aspects of Modern Poetry.*

'The true … mistake lies in the confounding mechanical regularity with organic form. The form is mechanic, when on any given material we impress a predetermined form, not necessarily arising out of the properties of the material; as when to a mass of wet clay we give whatever shape we wish it to retain when hardened. The organic form, on the other hand, is innate; it shapes as it develops, itself from within, and the fullness of its development is one and the same with … its outward form.'—Coleridge, *Lectures* (1818).

'For of the soul the body form doth take;
For soul is form, and doth the body make.'

SPENSER, 'Hymn in Honour of Beauty'

'To speak ... with the perfect rectitude and insouciance of the movements of animals, and the unimpeachableness of the sentiment of trees in the woods and grass by the roadside, is the flawless triumph of art. If you have looked on him who has achieved it, you have looked on one of the greatest masters of all nations and times. You shall not contemplate the flight of the grey gull across the bay, or the mettlesome action of the blood-horse, or the tall leaning of sunflowers on their stalk, or the appearance of the sun journeying through heaven, or the appearance of the moon afterward, with any more satisfaction than you shall contemplate him.'—WHITMAN, Preface to *Leaves of Grass*.

'No work of true genius dares want its appropriate form, neither indeed is there any danger of this. As it must not, so genius cannot, be lawless; for it is ever this that constitutes its genius—the power of acting creatively under laws of its own origination.'—COLERIDGE, *Lectures* (1818).

7. On Harmony and Proportion

'The world is made by symmetry and proportion, and is in that respect compared to music, and music to poetry ... what music can there be where there is no proportion observed.'—T. CAMPION, *Observations on the Art of English Poesie*.

'Harmony itself is a thing of thought.'—WAGNER, *Prose Works*, Chapter IV, Part III.

In other words, there must be no division between the thought and the clothing flesh, the harmony.—E. S.

'Harmony and Proportion are Qualities and not Things. The Harmony and Proportion of a Horse are not the same with those of a Bull. Every Thing has its own Harmony and Proportion, Two Inferior Qualities in it. For its Reality is its Imaginative Form.'—BLAKE, annotations to Berkeley's *Siris*.

Consider this saying of Blake's, young men. All spiritual Imagination is not fitted for the Harmony and Proportion of a Sonnet.

The swiftness of the Horse is not to be found in the Harmony and Proportion of a Sonnet.—E. S.

8. On Style

'His' (Wordsworth's) 'remark was by far the weightiest thing we ever heard on the subject of style; and it was this: that it is in the highest degree unphilosophic to call language the *dress* of thoughts. … He would call it the '*incarnation* of thoughts'. Never in one word was so profound a truth conveyed. … And the truth is apparent on consideration: for if language were merely a dress, then you could separate the two; you could lay the thoughts on the left hand, the language on the right. But, generally speaking, you can no more deal thus with poetic thoughts than you can with soul and body. The union is too subtle, the intertexture too ineffable.'—DE QUINCEY, *Style*.

'… Descartes has only ideas, and no visible style. His thought has a skin which clings to the flesh—not a flowered dress. This is equally true of Pascal. Their style is naked, sometimes sweating with fever, yellow from fasting, or suddenly red from the blood that has fled from the heart, leaving it turned to ice. It is naked as a soul.'—DE GOURMONT, *Le Problème du Style*.

'The living language of dream, the dead language of awakening. We need an interpreter, a translator.'—COCTEAU, *Opium*. Trans. Ernest Boyd.

9. On Technical Experiments

'... every great poet must inevitably innovate upon the example of his predecessors in the exact structure of his peculiar versification.'—SHELLEY, *A Defence of Poetry*.

Many and varied are the experimental enquiries made by modern poets into the effect on rhythm, and on speed, of the use of rhymes, assonances, and dissonances, placed outwardly, at different places in the line, in most elaborate patterns; and the effect on speed of equivalent syllables, that system which produces almost more variation than any other device.

The rhythm and speed of a skilful unrhymed poem differ from the rhythm and speed of a rhymed poem containing the same number of feet,—and both the rhymed and the unrhymed poems differ slightly in rhythm and speed from a poem ending with assonances or dissonances, but containing the same number of feet. Again, assonances and dissonances put at different places within the lines and intermingled with equally skilfully placed internal rhymes, have an immense effect upon rhythm and speed; and their effect on rhythm, and sometimes, but not always, upon speed, is different from that of lines containing elaborately schemed internal rhymes without assonances or dissonances.—E. S.

*   *   *

How slight, how subtle, are the changes in speed or of depth in English poetry, due to the fact that the English, in their cunning over the matter of poetry, have adopted the system of equivalence. For is it really to be supposed that two words of one syllable each, equal in speed one word of two syllables? The two-syllabled words, if unweighted by heavy consonants, move far more quickly. The system, therefore, of equivalent syllables gives variation.—E. S., *Alexander Pope*.

Sometimes, in the actual texture, subtle variations of thickness and thinness (and consequently of darkness or faint shadow) are brought about in assonances and rhymes by the changing of a consonant or labial, from word to word.

(On this subject, see page 136, note on Iachimo's speech.)

This change from thickness to thinness can actually affect, very faintly and subtly, rhythm and speed.

I have made innumerable experiments of each of the above kinds. Indeed, my verses *Façade* and certain other poems are, in a very great many cases, experiments of these orders.—E. S.

It must not be thought, however, that all matters of form derived from texture are superimposed,—are planned or deliberated by the poet: they are the result of instinct, and arise from the necessities of the material.—E. S.

Schopenhauer, in *The World as Will and Idea*, wrote: '(Nature) accomplishes that which appears so designed and planned, without reflection and without conception of an end. ... The six equal radii of a snowflake, separating at equal angles, are measured beforehand by no knowledge; but it is the simple tendency of the original Will, which exhibits itself to knowledge when knowledge appears.'

The poet accomplishes his design instinctively, but at the same time with knowledge. In him, knowledge has become instinct, and during the conception of the poem, knowledge works in him as if it were nature alone.

When the work is almost completed, when the inspiration has pronounced its will, then, and only then, does the knowledge become conscious knowledge once again.

The difference between the poet and the person who is not a poet, although he may (and no doubt does) write reams of verse, lies partly in the fact that the poet has this instinctive knowledge.—E. S.

10. Applicable to Free Verse

Orlando Gibbons, the composer, in a dedicatory address to Sir Christopher Hatton the younger, wrote, 'It is Proportion that beautifies everything'.

This should be remembered.—E. S.

Rhythm has been defined as 'Melody stripped of its pitch'.
This should be remembered.—E. S.

'The Impressionist school substitutes sunshine for light, and sonority for rhythm.'—COCTEAU ('Le Coq et l'Arlequin'), *Le Rappel à l'Ordre*.

Free Verse does not substitute sunshine for light, but it does, to a certain degree, substitute sonority for rhythm.—E. S.

Wagner wrote of Palestrina (*Beethoven*), 'Here rhythm is only perceptible through changes in the harmonic succession of chords, while apart from these it does not exist at all as a symmetrical division of time. Here the successions in time (*Zeitfolge*) are so immediately connected with the essential nature of harmony, which is itself connected with time and space, that the laws of time cannot aid us to understand such music. The sole succession of time in music of this description is hardly otherwise apparent than in exceedingly delicate changes of the same fundamental colour, which changes retain their connection through the most, varied transitions, without our being able to trace any direct drawing of lines.'

Is not this applicable to some of the verse of our time,—verse in which the shaping is not architectural, but is the result of the inward movement brought about by the texture, and particularly by the vowels … *i.e.* the 'exceedingly delicate changes of some fundamental colour'?—E. S.

Swinburne, writing of Rossetti (*Essays and Studies*), said that his line was 'as sinuous as water or as light, flexible and penetrative, delicate and rapid; it works on its way without halt, or jolt or collapse'.

Should this not be true of the line in Free Verse?—E. S.

Free Verse should have 'an astonishing sense of linear rhythm, a rhythm which is … extremely elastic, that is to say it is capable of extraordinary variations from the norm without loss of continuity. … Imagine the rhythm rendered the least bit tight and mechanical in its regularity, and the whole system … would break down.'—ROGER FRY, *Matisse*.

Young men, beware. Whitman described himself as 'apparently lawless; but on closer examination a certain regularity appears, like the recurrence of lesser and larger waves on the sea-shore, rolling without intermission, and fitfully rising and falling'.—WHITMAN, *Notebooks*.

I would like a strong and lovely movement—a movement belonging to the morning, the rush onward of

'Horses, young horses, and the waves of the sea.'

I do not know who wrote that wonderful phrase, nor where I found it.—E. S.

11. On Rhyme

'The profit of Rhyme is that it drops seeds of a sweeter and more luxuriant rhyme; and of uniformity, that it conveys itself into its own roots in the ground out of sight. The rhyme and uniformity of perfect poems show the free growth of metrical laws, and bud from them as unerringly and loosely as lilacs or roses on a bush, and take shapes as compact as the shapes of chestnuts and oranges and melons and pears, and shed the perfume impalpable to form.'—WHITMAN, Preface to *Leaves of Grass*.

'... the accident of a rhyme calls forth a system from the shadow.'—H. POINCARÉ, quoted by Cocteau ('Le Secret Professionnel'), *Le Rappel à l'Ordre*.
And a whole planetary system.—E. S.

12. On the Sonnet

'The irregular in the regular, the lack of correspondence in symmetry—what could be more illogical or more thwarting? Every infraction of the rule disturbs us like a false or doubtful note in music. The Sonnet is a sort of poetic fugue of which the theme should pass and repass until it is resolved according to its determined form. We must, therefore, submit ourselves absolutely to the laws of the Sonnet, or else, if we find those laws superannuated, pedantic, and restricting, abandon the writing of Sonnets.'—THÉOPHILE GAUTIER,

'Charles Baudelaire'—attached as a Preface to Baudelaire's *Les Fleurs du Mal.*

'False or doubtful note?' Gautier was not decrying strangeness, or the use of the unexpected sound by a musician. He was speaking of the false note played by the amateur in music.—E. S.

IV

On a Necessity of Poetry:
The Centre, the Core

'The hero is he who is immovably centred' (Emerson, quoted by Baudelaire, in *The Work and Life of Eugène Delacroix*). 'This', says Baudelaire, 'can equally be applied to the domain of poetry and art. The literary hero—that is to say the true writer, is he who is immovably centred. ... It is not surprising, then, that Delacroix has a very pronounced sympathy for those writers who are concise and concentrated, those whose prose, laden with but few ornaments, has the air of imitating the rapid movements of thought, and whose phrase resembles a gesture.'

'That which marks most visibly the style of Delacroix, is the conciseness, and a species of intensity without ostentation, the result of the habitual concentration of all his spiritual forces upon a given point.'—BAUDELAIRE, *ibid*.

'It is … a metre-making argument that makes a poem,—a thought so passionate and alive that, like the spirit of a plant or an animal, it has an architecture of its own, and adorns nature with a new thing.'—EMERSON ('The Poet'), *Essays*.

Blake said: 'A Spirit and a Vision are not, as the modern philosophy supposes, a cloudy vapour or a nothing: they are organised and minutely articulated beyond all that the mortal and perishing nature can produce. He who does not imagine in stronger and better lineaments, and in stronger and better light than his perishing and mortal eye can see, does not imagine at all.'— (*Descriptive Catalogue*).

V

On Morality in Poetry

'… We shall find a mere philosophy of morals without explanation of nature, such as Socrates wished to introduce … analogous to melody without harmony, which Rousseau desired exclusively; and contrariwise, mere Physics and Metaphysics without Ethics would be equivalent to harmony without melody.'—SCHOPENHAUER ('On the Metaphysics of Music'), quoted in Wagner's *Beethoven*. Trans. E. Dannreuther.

Never was a more valuable statement made. In addition to this harmony and melody, we need, as Emerson said ('Uses of Great Men', *Representative Men*), 'fire enough to fuse the mountain of ore—E. S.

VI

On Simplicity

'As a man raises himself towards Heaven, so his view of the spiritual world becomes simplified and his words fewer.'—DIONYSIUS THE AREOPAGITE, *Mystical Theology*.

The best poetry of our time, although it is held to be of an extreme complication, has actually attained to a new kind of simplicity and compression. That so much of a varying character should be compressed into a line is startling, because it involves the fusion of exceedingly complicated cross-currents and cross-lights into an element.

It is only by attaining to this fusion, that poetry becomes 'the voice of the world'.—E. S.

To attain to this simplicity, involves the problem of becoming our subject.—E. S. 'Everything that is not believed remains decorative.'—COCTEAU, *Opium*. Trans. Ernest Boyd. 'It is a question of the painter who likes to paint trees becoming a tree.'—EMERSON, quoted by Cocteau, in *Opium*. Trans. Ernest Boyd.

40

'The Beautiful is invariably of a double composition, in spite of the fact that the impression it makes is single; for the difficulty of discerning the varying elements of beauty in the unity of the impression, in no way invalidates the need for variety in the composition. The Beautiful is composed of an eternal, invariable element, of a quantity difficult to determine, and of a relative, circumstantial element, which may be the epoch, the mode, ethics, or passion (either alternatively, or together). Without this second element … the first element would be indigestible, unappreciable, not adapted or appropriate to human nature.'—BAUDELAIRE, *L'Art Romantique.*

'What is style? For many people, a very complicated way of saying very simple things. According to us, a very simple way of saying very complicated things.'—COCTEAU ('Le Secret Professionnel') *Le Rappel à l'Ordre.*

'Satie invents a new simplicity. The transparent air undresses the lines. Pain does not grimace.'—COCTEAU ('Carte Blanche'), *Le Rappel à l'Ordre.*

'A true poet does not trouble about the poetical. In the same way as a horticulturist does not scent his roses. He makes them follow a system that perfects their cheeks and their breath.'— COCTEAU ('Le Secret Professionnel'), *Le Rappel à l'Ordre.*

'Simplicity changes sides. That which is simple, is the mass, the unformed. That which is composed, is the element.

'The elementary form reveals itself as polymorphous and iridescent.

'Often unity scintillates.'—GASTON BACHELARD, *Irrationalism:* appeared in the review *Minotaure.*

'One need only look closely at a drawing by Ingres, to see that it sparkles with little touches, chips from the spiritual mine. Yet they speak of Ingres as if they were seeing a pure line.'—COCTEAU ('Le Coq et l'Arlequin'), *Le Rappel à l'Ordre*.

Simplicity is not paucity.—E. S.

'The Greek temple is beautiful because taste has banished from it the superfluous. The sky-scraper is beautiful because utility has banished from it the superfluous. These beauties are antipodal, but the antipodes resemble each other.'—COCTEAU ('Carte Blanche'), *Le Rappel à l'Ordre*.

'Machinery and American sky-scrapers resemble Greek Art, in the sense that utility bestows on them a dryness and a grandeur deprived of the superfluous. But that is not art. The rôle of art is to seize the sense of the epoch and extract from the contemplation of this practical aridity an antidote to the beauty of the useless, which encourages superfluity.'—*Ibid*.

A valuable example of modern simplicity and compression occurs in the scene in Cocteau's *Orphé'e*, in which Orpheus and Eurydice have returned from Hades. This scene, however, is in prose, not verse:

'EURYDICE: If you knew how unimportant are these "histoires"'—(scenes about? stories about—the word can mean either.—E. S.) 'the moon and the sun.

'ORPHEUS: Madame is above such things.

'EURYDICE: If I could only speak …'

VII

On the Senses

'The Four Senses are the Four Faces of Man & the Four Rivers of the Water of Life.'—BLAKE, annotations to Berkeley's *Siris*.

The poet's mind has become a central sense, interpreting and controlling the other five senses; (E. S.) for we have rediscovered the truth uttered by Blake, that 'Man has no Body distinct from his soul, for that called Body is a portion of Soul discern'd by the five Senses, the chief inlets of Soul in this age'.—BLAKE, *Marriage of Heaven and Hell.*

'By the very right of your senses you enjoy the world. Is not the beauty of the Hemisphere present 'to your eye? Doth not the glory of the Sun pay tribute to your sight? Is not the vision of 'the world an amiable thing? Do not the stars shed influences to perfect the Air? ... Prize these first, and you shall enjoy the residues: Glory, Dominion, Power, Wisdom, Honour, Angels, Souls, Kingdoms. ...'—TRAHERNE, *Centuries of Meditation.*

'… it is asserted, that God invented and bestowed sight on us for this purpose, that, on surveying the circles of intelligence in the heavens, we might properly employ those of our own minds, which, though disturbed when compared with the others that are uniform, are still allied to their circulations; and that, having thus learned, and being naturally possessed of a correct reasoning faculty, we might, by imitating the uniform revolutions of divinity, set right our own wanderings and blunders.'—PLATO, *Timaeus*.

'By experiments of Sense we become acquainted with the lower faculties of the Soul, and from them, whether by a gradual evolution or ascent, we arrive at the highest.'—BERKELEY, *Siris*: quoted by Blake, *Marginalia*.

'The inmost kernel of all genuine and actual knowledge is a perception; and every new truth is the profit or gain yielded by a perception. … Merely abstract thoughts, which have no kernel of perception, are the cloud-structures, without reality.

'Wisdom and genius, those two summits of the Parnassus of human knowledge, have their foundation not in the abstract and discursive, but in the perceptive faculty; Wisdom proper is something intuitive, not something abstract. It does not consist in principles and thoughts which one can carry about ready in his mind.'—SCHOPENHAUER, *The World as Will and Idea*. Trans. R. B. Haldane and J. Kemp.

'Helvétius forced on Rimbaud the conception of the mind as the product of the senses, which, to one of such sensual activity as Rimbaud, gave great comfort. Even Memory, Helvétius demonstrated, is simply a continuation of sensation, weakened but conserved, so that the mind, whether in itself it be material or not, is completely the product of the nervous sensibility.

'One of the examples chosen by Helvétius to illustrate his theory is the low mentality of animals such as the horse. The extremities of these creatures, their hoofs, are covered with insensitive horn, and if we consider how much knowledge we owe to the delicacy of our hands, the reasoning of Helvétius appears most plausible. This, I imagine, was the starting point of Helvétius' reasoning: "Let us refine our fingers, that is *all* our points of contact with the external world, and all our minds will become proportionally superior to those of ordinary men, as theirs are now to horses'"."'—EDGELL RICKWARD, *Rimbaud: The Boy and the Poet.*

'The poet makes himself a seer by a long, immense, and reasoned unruliness of all his senses.'—RIMBAUD, Letter to Delahaye, 1872.

This is only true of a certain kind of poetry. But it is true that where the language of one sense is insufficient, we use that appertaining to another.—E. S.

VIII

On Over-Civilisation

'We have just passed through a long period of error in art, caused by the knowledge of physical and mechanical chemistry, and by the study of nature. Artists having lost their savagery, and no longer able to rely upon instinct, one might better say imagination, have strayed off on so many different paths to find the productive elements they no longer have the strength to create; and now they cannot work except in disorderly crowds, feeling frightened, almost lost, if left to themselves.'—GAUGUIN, *Letters*. Trans. Ruth Pielkova.

'I have found that in the composition of the human body as compared with the bodies of animals, the organs of sense are duller and coarser. Thus it is composed of less ingenuous instruments, and of spaces less capacious for receiving the faculties of sense. I have seen in the Lion Tribe that the sense of smell is connected with part of the substance of the brain which comes down from the nostrils.'—LEONARDO DA VINCI, *Note-books*.

46

'The eyes in the Lion Tribe have a larger part of the head for their sockets, and the optic nerves communicate at once with the brain; but the contrary is to be seen in Man, for the sockets of the eyes are but a small part of the head, and the optic nerves are very fine and long.'—*Ibid.*

We must have the eyes, the nose, of the Lion, the Lion's acuity of sense, and with these, the Sun of Man's reason.

Remember the 'animal full of genius', of whom Baudelaire wrote. (See page 4.)— E. S.

'... of this great personage Pan we have a very particular description in the ancient writers, who unanimously agree to represent him ... hairy all over, half a man and half a beast. ...

'Since the chief thing to which he applied himself was the civilising of mankind ... it should seem that the first principle of science must be received from that nation to which the gods were by Homer said to resort twelve days every year for the conversation of its wise and just inhabitants.'—Martin Scriblerus, *On the Origin of Sciences.*

'... In all the western parts of the world there was a great and memorable era in which they' (the beast-philosophers) 'began to be silent. ... Men's heads became too much puzzled to receive the simpler wisdom of these ancient Sylvans.'—*Ibid.*

IX

The Need for the Refreshing
of the Language

'Their' (the poets') 'language is vitally metaphorical; that is, it marks the before unapprehended relations of things and perpetuates their apprehension, until the words which represent them become, through time, signs for portions or classes of thoughts instead of pictures of integral thoughts; and then if no new poets should arise to create afresh the associations which have been thus disorganised, language will be dead to all the nobler purposes of human intercourse. These similitudes or relations are finely said by Lord Bacon to be "the same footsteps of nature impressed upon the various subjects of the world" (*De Augment. Scient.* Cap. I, Lib. III)—and he considers the faculty which perceives them as the storehouse of axioms common to all knowledge.'—SHELLEY, *A Defence of Poetry*.

X

On the Poets Labour

'PRAYER is the Study of Art,
Praise is the Practice of Art.'
BLAKE, sentences engraved above the plate of the Laocoon
Group.

XI

On Imagery in Poetry

'The rise, the setting of imagery, should, like the sun, come natural to him' (the reader), 'shine over him, and set soberly, although in magnificence, leaving him in the luxury of twilight.'—KEATS, *Letters*.

'… those ornaments can be allowed that conform to the perfect facts of the open air, and that flow out of the nature of the work, and come irrepressibly from it, and are necessary to the completion of the work.'—WHITMAN, Preface to *Leaves of Grass*.

(After a comparison of poetry to a ship, and poets to a mariner) '… some, to goe the lighter away, will take in their fraught of spangled feathers, golden Peebles, Straw, Reedes, Bulrushes or anything, and then they heave out their sayles as proudly as if they were balisted with Bulbecfe.'—THOMAS NASHE, Preface to the first quarto edition (1591) of Sidney's *Astrophel and Stella*.

XII

On the Poet, the Natural World, and Inspiration

'The Heat, Light, and Atmospheres of the Natural World only open Seeds; and this not by Powers derived from their own Sun, but by Powers from the spiritual Sun ... for the Image of Creation is Spiritual; nevertheless, that it may appear, and furnish use in the natural world ... it must be clothed in Matter.'—SWEDENBORG, *Wisdom of Angels Concerning Divine Love and Divine Wisdom*: quoted in Blake's *Marginalia*.

'Often before dawn', said Goethe, 'I am awake, and lie down by the open window to enjoy the splendour of the three planets at present visible together, and to refresh myself with the increasing brilliance of the morning-red. I then pass almost the whole day in the open air, and hold spiritual communion with the tendrils of the vine, which say good things to me, and of which I could tell you wonders.'—Conversations of Goethe with Eckermann.

'When I see where the east is greater than the west … or a father is more needful than a mother to produce me—then I guess I shall see how spirit is greater than matter.'—WHITMAN, *Notebooks*.

'The soul or spirit transcends itself into all matter,—into rocks, and can live the life of a rock—into the sea, and can feel itself the sea … into the earth—into the motions of the suns and stars.

'Never speak of the soul as anything but intrinsically great. The effusion or corporation of the soul is always under the beautiful laws of physiology.'—*Ibid*.

XIII

On the Power of Words

'I am not yet so lost in lexicography, as to forget that words are the daughters of earth, and that things are the sons of heaven.'—DR. JOHNSON, Preface to *Dictionary of the English Language.*

William Rossetti, in his Foreword to Whitman's *Leaves of Grass*, says: 'Whitman's language has a certain ultimate quality'.

It is this 'ultimate quality' in language,—and 'speech above a mortal mouth', to quote from Ben Jonson's *Discoveries*—that is needed in the poetry of to-day.—E. S.

'... The grammar, the arid grammar itself, becomes something like an evoked sorcery, the words are alive again in flesh and in blood, the substantive, in its substantial majesty, the adjective, a transparent vestment that clothes and colours it ... and the verb, angel of movement.'—BAUDELAIRE, *Les Paradis Artificiels.* Trans, and quoted by Arthur Symons.

Furious old lady, complaining of my own poems: 'Words, Words, nothing but Words'.

Not *only* words, my dear lady. Yet see what only words will do for us. Compare these lines,

> 'And we'll gang nae mair a-rovin,
> A rovin in the nicht,'

from 'The Jolly Beggar', by James V of Scotland, and the final lines of Byron's 'We'll go no more a-roving', a poem that begins with lines which are almost those of King James, but ends with

> 'Yet we'll go no more a-roving
> By the light of the moon.'

—E. S.

XIV

Of the Deaths of Two Poets

Shelley, in a letter to Mary, September 22, 1818:
    'Am I not like a wild swan to be gone so suddenly?'
    Was the wild swan thinking of that flight that was so near?—
E. S.

Thomas Nashe, in his Preface to Sidney's 'Astrophel and Stella':
    'Deare Astrophel, that in the ashes of thy Love livest againe
like the Phoenix.'

XV

Of Ben Jonson

'If', says Professor Saintsbury (*History of Prosody*), 'we were playing the old children's game of "Animal, Vegetable or Mineral "in respect of Jonson's prosody, I should say about his lyrics "Animal", and of all but the very highest animation; of his couplets "Vegetable", and first-rate Vegetable; but of his blank verse, "Mineral": weighty, sometimes brilliant, but not alive.'

I do not think that all the lyrics of Jonson come under the heading of 'Animal'; some, for instance, grow like a flower, from the soil, but with the clear beauty of a flower. 'The Sad Shepherd' has a fresh and invigorating, shaggy, forestial roughness,—'hairy' language, as Dante would have said. But Professor Saintsbury's qualifications are useful.—E. S.

XVI

Applicable to the Augustans

'… the dry light which did scorch and offend most men's natures.'—BACON, *Essays*, quoted by Emerson.

'Architecture' … (brings to) 'greater distinctness some of those ideas which are the lowest grade of the objectivity of the Will; such as gravity, cohesion, rigidity, hardness, those universal qualities of stone, those first, simplest, most inarticulate manifestments of Will: the base notes of Nature.'—SCHOPENHAUER ('Architecture'), *The World as Will and Idea*.

NOTE.—In this, Augustan poetry, as I have remarked elsewhere, bears a strong resemblance to Architecture; not only because of its rigid outward structure (which contains, however, within the lines, from pole to pole, great variation)—but because the consonantal system, the mass of the planet (see Note on Dunbar), is the base of those inward variations.—E. S.

XVII

Some Notes on Alexander Pope

1. Of his Personal Character

'Of his personal character' (Swinburne, *A Century of English Poetry*) 'it is nothing to say that he had the courage of a lion: for a beast's or an athlete's courage must have something of physical force to back it: something of a body to base itself upon: and the spirit which was in Pope, we might say, was almost as good as bodiless. And what a spirit it was! How fiery bright and dauntless!

'We are invited, and not always unreasonably, to condone or palliate much that was unworthy of manhood in Byron, on just and compassionate consideration of the bitter burden attached to his bodily and daily life; but what was his trial and what was his courage to Pope's? how less than little the one, how less than nothing the other! For Byron we should have charity and sympathy: but it rouses the blood, it kindles the heart, to remember what an indomitable force of heroic spirit, and sleepless always as fire, was enclosed in the pitiful body of the misshapen weakling whose whole life was spent in fighting the good fight of sense against folly, of light against darkness, of human speech against brute silence, of truth and reason and manhood against all the banded bestialities. ...'

2. Of the Perfection of Pope

'Whatever Pope has left us is as round and smooth as Giotto's "O", whatever Dryden has left us is liable to come short of this empirical and precious praise. The strength of Dryden never wholly fails him, but the skill of Pope never fails him at all.'— SWINBURNE, *ibid.*

3. Applicable to the Work of Pope

Wagner, on the subject of Mozart (*Prose Works)*, wrote 'with him grey was always grey and red red; only that this grey and this red were equally bathed with the freshening dew of his music, were resolved into all the nuances of the primordial colour, and thus appeared as many-tinted grey, as many-tinted red'.

4. Of the Technical Side of Pope's Work

Actually melody was absent from the poems of Pope, in spite of their technical splendour and unsurpassed flawlessness,—and this lack is due to their unvaried outward structure. For to produce melody, in spite of the variations caused by texture, those variations are not alone sufficient. We must also have variations in the outward structure; and it was to this that we were restored by Shelley, Blake, and Coleridge.

It must be remembered, however, that melody is not the only technical or oral joy to be gained from poetry.—E. S.

5. Of the Heroic Couplet

'The heroic couplet, which is kept strictly within the limits of its outward structure, is yet as variable within those limits as waves, as the air with its light variations of wind, indeed, as variable as the earth itself with its mountains and plains. The reason why, to an insensitive ear, the heroic couplet seems monotonous, is because structure alone, and not texture, has been regarded as the maker of rhythm.'—E. S., *Alexander Pope*.

6. Of Pope's Sense of Texture

'He stated repeatedly that everything he knew about versification he learned from Dryden, and that even at the age of twelve he could distinguish the difference between softness and sweetness in the texture of the several poets; for his feeling for this most important matter of texture was so phenomenally sensitive that had the verses been transformed into flowers, he could have told lily from rose, buttercup from cowslip, in no matter how starless and moonless the night, merely by touching one petal. In these matters, he found Dryden to be softer, Waller sweeter; and that the same difference, the same subtle distinction, separated Ovid from Vergil.'—E. S., *Alexander Pope*.

I presume he was referring to such poems of Dryden's as 'Annus Mirabilis' and 'Ode to Mrs. Anne Killigrew'. He could not, of course, have referred to the satires.

XVIII

A Note on Byron

Swinburne wrote: 'Byron … was supreme in his turn—a king by truly divine right, but in a province outside the proper domain of absolute poetry'.

This is true of nearly all Byron's poetry, yet what a wonder is 'We'll go no more a-roving',—a wonder, surely, even in the 'domain of absolute poetry'. And I do not know, of its own kind, a more superb monument of grief than the last five lines in the ultimate stanza of 'And thou art dead, as young and fair':

> 'The all of thine that cannot die
> Through dark and dread Eternity
>   Returns again to me,
> And more thy buried love endears
> Than aught except its living years.'

Is not this great poetry? I think that it is. There is no falsehood here.—And much of the rest of the poem is deeply moving,

61

though not quite on that level. The two lines

> 'We'll go no more a-roving
>> By the light of the moon'

are, again, wonderful poetry.

XIX

Applicable to Blake

Schopenhauer, in *The World as Will and Idea*, spoke of 'the naïveté with which every plant expresses and lays open its whole character in its mere form, reveals its whole being and will. This is why the physiognomy of plants is so interesting. ... The plant reveals its whole being at the first glance, and with complete innocence. ... This innocence in the plant results from its complete want of knowledge. ... Every plant speaks to us, first of all, of its home, of the climate, and the nature of the ground in which it has grown. ... Besides this, however, every plant expresses the special will of its species, and says something that cannot be uttered in any other tongue.'

Blake had the innocence of the flower, but his innocence did not come from ignorance, but from wisdom. The extreme poles, want of knowledge, and wisdom, are alike.—E. S.

'It is the supreme quality of this wisdom that it has never let go of intuition. It is as if intuition itself ripened.'—ARTHUR SYMONS, *William Blake*.

'At the birth of Blake—to paraphrase a sentence in Rimbaud's "Fairy"' (*Les Illuminations*: trans. Helen Rootham), 'were present the saps of beauty in the untrodden shadows and the still radiancy of the astral silence.'—For his childhood, 'the thickets and the deep shadows trembled, the hearts of the poor and the legends of heaven were stirred.'

Blake, in a letter to Hayley (27 January 1804), wrote of verses that 'still sound upon my ear like the distant approach of things mighty and magnificent, like the sound of harps which I hear before the Sun's rising'.

Wonderful—and strange. He was speaking of verses by a poet of little, or no, worth. But might he not have been speaking of some of his own verses? Not all: not the *Songs of Innocence*, in which, as Gilchrist wrote in his Life of Blake, we hear 'an angelic voice singing to an oaten pipe'.—E. S.

Blake, in his own words, 'entered into Noah's rainbow, and made a friend and companion of one of those images of wonder. ...'

'Nothing can withstand the fury of my Course among the Sons of God & in the Abysses of the Accuser.'—BLAKE, Letter to Thomas Butts, Jan. 10, 1802.

'The root of all is God. But it is not the way to receive fruits to dig to the root, but to reach to the boughs. I reach for my creation to the Father, for my redemption to the Son, and for my sanctification to the Holy Ghost: and so I make the knowledge of God, a tree of life unto me, and not otherwise.'—DONNE, Sermon CIX, preached at Court, April 1629.

Such also was the wisdom of Blake.—E.S.

Blake might have said, with Smart (*Rejoice with the Lamb*), 'In my nature I quested for Beauty—but God, God hath sent me to the sea for pearls'.

To the salt, the bitter waters of affliction.—E. S.

'In heaven the angels are advancing continually to the spring-time of their youth, so that the oldest angel appears the young-est.'—SWEDENBORG, quoted by Emerson ('Swedenborg, or the Mystic'), *Representative Men*.

This might have been said of Blake in his old age.—E. S.

XX

Applicable to Baudelaire

'Happy, happy they that in Hell feel not the world's despite.'— The last words written by Dowland for *Lachrimae, or Seven Teares, figured in Seven Passionate Pavanes.*

'Could we not believe ourselves in Palmyra unruined. ...'— Théophile Gautier, *Charles Baudelaire* (attached as a Preface to *Les Fleurs du Mal*).

(Note.—'Intact' was the word in French—it seems unsuitable in English.—E. S.)

'A profound light that the ear fathoms without fatigue ...' (a work of art) 'vegetable and architectural as a banana-tree of Rio.'—Cocteau, writing of a work by Milhaud ('Carte Blanche'), *Le Rappel à l'Ordre.*

This saying of Cocteau's might equally apply to certain works of Baudelaire's, although Milhaud's music would seem to bear no relation to Baudelaire's strange spirit.—E. S.

'… I was once told by a near relative of mine, that having in her childhood fallen into a river, and being on the very verge of death … she saw in a moment her whole life, clothed in its forgotten incidents, arrayed before her … not successively, but simultaneously; and she had a faculty developed as suddenly for comprehending the whole and every part.'—DE QUINCEY, *Confessions of an English Opium-Eater*.

It is this simultaneity, a kind of water-clearness (into which he fell as into a river) on the verge of death, to which Baudelaire has attained.—E. S.

'This poet … loved what one wrongly calls the style of decadence, which is no other thing than the arrival of art at this extreme point of maturity that determined in their oblique suns the civilisations that aged; a style ingenious, complicated, learned, full of shades and of rarities, turning for ever backward the limits of the language, using technical vocabularies, taking colour from all the palettes, notes from all the keyboards. … In regard to his verse there is the language already veined in the greenness of decomposition, the tainted language of the later Roman Empire, and the complicated refinements of the Byzantine School, the last form of Greek Art fallen in delinquencies.'—THÉOPHILE GAUTIER, *Charles Baudelaire*. Quoted and translated by Arthur Symons in *Baudelaire, a Study*.

'Polysyllabic and ample-sounding words are pleasing to Baudelaire, and with three or four of these words, he often makes verses which seem immense and in which these vibrating sounds prolong the measure.'—THÉOPHILE GAUTIER, *Charles Baudelaire*. Trans. E. S.

His 'great Alexandrines … come, in a time of calm, to die on the shore with the tranquil and profound undulation of the wave arriving from the open sea'.—*Ibid.*

XXI

Applicable to Verlaine

'Sometimes in a kind of melting jargon of the countryside, he spoke of death which brings repentance, of the unhappy, of painful labours, of partings that rend the heart. In the hovels where we used to get drunk he wept while he contemplated those who surrounded us, Poverty's cattle. He raised up drunkards in the foul streets. He had the compassion of a wicked mother for little children.'—ARTHUR RIMBAUD, *A Season in Hell*. Trans. Helen Rootham.

'I felt an extreme pleasure this morning, on seeing again a little picture of mine. There was nothing in it, but it was charming and seemed as if it had been painted by a bird.'—Letter from COROT, quoted in *Opium*, by Jean Cocteau. Trans. Ernest Boyd.

This would be true of Verlaine, were he spiritually evil, instead of pure:

'Only a bird could trust itself to paint the Profanation of the Host. Only a bird could be pure enough, selfish enough, cruel enough.'—Jean Cocteau, *Opium*. Trans. Ernest Boyd.

Applicable to Certain Poems of Verlaine.

'I know several sculptures of Giacometti which are so solid, so light, that they look like snow on which a bird has left its footmarks.'—*Ibid*.

'… aspects of people and things in which a butterfly seems to have left a little of its coloured dust as it alights and pauses.'—Arthur Symons on Whistler, *Studies in Seven Arts*.

'… They have their brief coloured life like butterflies, and with the same momentary perfection.'—Arthur Symonson Whistler and Verlaine, *ibid*.

'A white which is like the soul of a colour caught and fixed there by some incalculable but precisely coloured magic. It ends, of course, by being the ghost of a colour … but all things end, when their particular life is over, by becoming the ghost of themselves.'—Arthur Symons on Whistler, *ibid*.

Dr. D. S. MacColl, in his *19th Century Painting*, said of Manet that his mind is 'that joyful, heedless mind of summer, beneath or above thought, the intense sensation of life, with its lights and colours, coming and going in the head'.

'Words serve him with so absolute a negation that he can write *Romances sans Paroles*—songs almost without words, in which scarcely a sense of the interference of human speech remains.'—Arthur Symons, *The Symbolist Movement in French Literature*.

'He created in verse a new voice for nature, full of the humble ecstasy with which he saw, listened and accepted … and with the same attentive simplicity with which he found words for the sensations of hearing and the sensations of sight, he found words for the sensations of the soul, for the fine shades of feeling. ... Here ... are words which startle one by their delicate resemblance to thoughts, by their winged flight from so far, by their alighting so close.'—*Ibid*.

XXII

A Note on the Earliest English Poetry

The earliest English poetry of all, with its crude and unskilled thumping, or creaking, alliteration, echoes the sound of those earthy occupations which accompany the work of food-getting.

The creaking and thumping of the waggons, 'the sharp sound of the flail threshing the corn, sound even in devotional poems, as in this excerpt from 'The Orison of Our Lady', a poem of which, says Saintsbury, 'we have no copy certainly older than 1200, but which cannot be much later than that date, and is probably much older':

> Christis milde moder seynte marie
> Mines liues leome mi leoue lefdi,
> To the ich buwe and mine kneon ich beie
> And al min heorte blod to the ich offree,
> Thu ert mire soule liht, and mine heorte blisse,
> Mi lif and mi tohope min heale mid iwisse,

Ich ouh wurthie the mid alle mine mihte,
And singge the lofsang bi daie and bi nihte
Vor thu me hauest iholpen aweole kunne wise,
And ibrouht (me) of helle into paradise.

XXIII

Notes on Chaucer

Blake said of Chaucer (*Descriptive Catalogue*): 'As Newton numbered the stars, and as Linneus numbered the plants, so Chaucer numbered the classes of men'.

*   *   *

Swinburne wrote of Ariosto that he 'threw across the windy sea of glittering legend and fluctuant romance the broad summer lightnings of his large and jocund genius'.

This might, in one sense, have been said equally of Chaucer, were it not that his movements are neither sharp, like those of lightning, nor fluctuant, like those of a sea.

Those fresh and shining poems *The Canterbury Tales* have a curiously strong and resilient line, an urgent life. Their strength is of nature, and the will which is in them, and which forms their purpose and guides their direction, is instinctive. Close to the earth as are these poems, often the strength and movement of the lines, for all the warmth and humanity in them, are like the strength and movement of a slow plant life.

Sometimes the line is divided by a pause that is both long and deep, but the two halves divided by the pause have a movement and impetus of a peculiar strength, and this is not the rushing, tumultuous swelling movement of the march of waves (for it is often slow, and it has more direction than that of waves); it has, rather, the inevitability and urgency of sap rising in a plant. At moments the growth is horizontal, its urgency keeps close to the earth, as with a melon (because the vowels are equal in length, in height, or in depth),—but more often, owing to a rising system of sharp vowels, it springs into the air, like sap rising in a tree.

A beautiful example of the *first* kind is the following song of Troilus,—'If no love is, O God, what fele I so?'—where some, but not all the lines are divided—in this case after the fourth syllable—by a stretching pause. The line then continues in its resistless way, in its plant-life,—(though, like the plant, it has its variations of leaves and flowers),—the other lines being undivided.—The levels of the earth are different, however, in the lines, and are sometimes uneven. Sometimes the vowels rise, and fall again; yet the lines stretch onwards, they do not soar.

> If no love is, O God, what fele I so?
> And if love is, what thing and which is he?
> If love be good, from whennes cometh my wo?
> If it be wikke, a wonder thynketh me,
> When every torment and adversite
> That cometh of him, may to me savory thinke;
> For ay thurst I, the more that ich it drinke.

And if that at myn owen lust I brenne,
Fro whennes cometh my wailing and my pleynte?
If harm agree me, wher-to pleyne I thenne?
I noot, ne why unwery that I feynte.
O quike deth, O swete harm so queynte,
How may of the in me swich quantite,
But if that I consente that it be?

And if that I consente, I wrongfully
Compleyne, y-wis; thus possed to and fro,
Al stereless with-inne a boot am I
Amydde the see, by-tuixen wyndes two,
That in contrarie stonden evere-mo.
Allas! what is this wonder maladye?
For hete of cold, for cold of hete, I dye.

The assonances, dissonances, and alliterations have much effect here,—'whennes', 'wikke', 'wonder',—'thynketh' echoing 'wikke';—the change, in the second verse, from 'myn' to 'pleyne', and the dulling from 'pleyne' to 'thenne'; the echo of 'wailing' and 'pleynte'—the first being long yet broken, the second dying away at once.

'An example of the second kind (the line whose impetus, owing to its vowel system, rises with a strong sharp strength) is the following magnificent line:

The mighty tresses in hir sonnish heres.

—I know, and have been reminded of the fact by correspondents, that the *o* in 'sonnish' was usually pronounced as the letter *u* is now pronounced in German. But variations were in use in the time of Chaucer, and I think that here is a case. If, then, 'sonnish' was pronounced as we now pronounce the word 'sun' each accented vowel-sound rises, sharply, after the other, springing upward. In this line, incidentally, there is no pause. Air, however, plays around the line, owing to the long vowels; it has not, therefore, as have many pauseless lines, a huddled quality.

Much of the variation in sound of this wonderful poetry is due (as I have said already) to the fact that some lines are divided sharply in two by a deep pause, whilst at other times there is no pause at all, or else several small pauses. An example is that miracle, the first rondel of 'Merciles Beaute'—to me the only perfect rondel in the English language:

> Your eyen two wol slee me sodenly,
> I may the beaute of hem not sustene,
> So woundeth hit through-out my herte kene.
>
> And but your word wol helen hastily
> My hertes wounde, why! that hit is grene,
> *Your eyen two wol slee me sodenly,*
> *I may the beaute of hem not sustene.*
>
> Upon my trouthe I sey yow feithfully,
> That ye ben of my lyf and deeth the quene;
> For with my deeth the trouthe shal be sene.
> Your eyen two wol slee me sodenly,
> *I may the beaute of hem not sustene,*
> *So woundeth hit through-out my herte kene.*

The English rondel is usually a giggling, trivial horror; but this poem has a most clear, noble, and grave beauty.

Turning from this, let us consider the variations, the peculiar softness and sweetness given by the pauses changing from line to line, in number, in length, in depth,—sometimes rising, sometimes stretching faintly outward, sometimes dropping), and, too, by the faint dissonances of 'softe' and 'cougheth', and the deeper dissonances of 'semysoun' and 'honeycomb' in these lines:

> And softe he cougheth with a semysoun:
> What do ye, hony-comb, sweete Alisoun,
> My faire bryd, my sweete cynamome.

Here the actual texture is affected by the pauses. Part of the beauty is due, also, to the marvellously managed, sweet s and c sounds, and to the fact that the second syllable of 'cynamome', coming after the high-vowelled first syllable, has a soft dropping movement.

Was that sweetness and softness the original inspiration, though not the subject, of this wonderful passage in James Joyce's *Ulysses*: 'And in New York a slack dishonoured body that once was comely, as sweet, as fresh, as cinnamon, now her leaves falling, all, bare, frighted of the narrow grave and unforgiven'?

Chaucer has been accused, by persons incapable of hearing subtleties of difference, of a lack of variety. But how great are the differences in these two fragments from 'Troilus and Criseyede':

> O sterre, of which I lost have al the light,
> With herte soor wel oughte I to biwaille,
> That evere derk in torment, nyght by nyght,
> Toward my deth with wind in steere I saille;
> For which the tenthe nyght, if that I faille,
> The gydyng of thi bemes bright an houre
> My ship and me Caribdis wol devoure.
>
> This song whan he thus songen hadde, soone
> He fel ayeyn into his sikkes olde.

In this wonderful fragment the vowels that are at once dark and shining, like water seen by clear moonlight (and this is not a matter of association only)—of 'sterre', 'herte', 'derk'—these assonances alternating with the faint cloudiness of the vowels in 'deth', 'tenthe',—these changing again to the long bright clear vowels of 'light', 'nyght', 'bright',—(and these latter are the high points of the scheme)—the handling of these assonances, and the alliterations, give a flawless beauty to the movement.

The consonants are never thick or heavy.

In the 'ardent harmony, the heat of spiritual life guiding the movement' of the second fragment quoted below, there is more body. This supreme magnificence is indeed a song of the morning.

PLESAUNCE OF LOVE

O blisful light, of whiche the bemes clere
Adorneth all the thridde hevene faire!
O sonnes lief, O Joves doughter dere,
Plesaunce of love, O goodly debonaire,
In gentil hertes ay redy to repaire!
O verray cause of hele and of gladnesse,
I-heried be thy myght and thy goodnesse!

In hevene and helle, in erthe and salte see
Is felt thi myght, if that I wel descerne;
As man, brid, best, fissh, herbe, and grene tree
Thee fele in tymes with vapour eterne.
God loveth, and to love wol nought werne;
And in this world no lyves creature
With-outen love is worth, or may endure.

Ye Joves first to thilke effectes glade,
Thorugh which that thynges liven alle and be,

Comeveden, and amorous him made
On mortal thing, and as yow list, ay ye
Yeve hym in love ese or adversitee;
And in a thousand formes doun hym sente
For love in erthe, and whom yow liste, he hente.

Ye fierse Mars apeysen of his ire,
And as yow list, ye maken hertes digne;
Algates, hem that ye wol sette a-fyre,
They dreden shame, and vices they resygne;
Ye do hem corteys be, fresshe and benigne,
And hye or lowe, after a wight entendeth,
The joies that he hath, youre myght him sendeth.

Ye holden regne and hous in unitee;
Ye sothfast cause of frendship ben also;
Ye knowe al thilke covered qualitee
Of things which that folk on wondren so,
Whan they can not construe how it may jo,
She loveth him, or whi he loveth here,
As whi this fissh, and nought that cometh to were.

Ye folk a lawe han set in universe;
And this knowe I by hem that lovers be,
That who-so stryveth with yow hath the werse:
Now, lady bright, for thi benignite,
At reverence of hem that serven the,
Whos clerk I am, so techeth me devyse
Som joye of that is felt in this servyse.

Ye in my naked herte sentement
Inhielde, and do me shewe of thy swetnesse.—
Caliope, thi vois be now present,

For now is nede; sestow not my destresse,
How I mot telle anon-right the gladnesse
Of Troilus, to Venus heryinge?
To which gladnes, who nede hath, God him bringe!

GLOSSARY.—*Hele*: health. *Werne*: refuse. *Thilke*: that same. *Comeveden:* didst instigate. *Yeve:* give. *Hente*: seized. *Algates:* in every way. *Jo:* how it may come about. *Were:* weir. *Inhielde:* pair in.

In another song of Troilus, 'O Cruel Day', the first two lines are deliberately harsh and cacophonous, with the hard, wooden, clacking sound of 'cock'. 'commune', and the 'crowe' of the second line. The whole passage is, deliberately, singularly harsh and dissonantal.

But whan the cok, comune astrologer,
Gan on his brest to bete and after crowe,
And Lucifer, the dayes messager,
Gan for to ryse, and out hire bemes throwe,
And estward roos, to hym that koude it knowe,
Fortuna Major, that anoon Criseyde,
With herte soor, to Troilus thus seyde:

'Myn hertes lif, my trist, and my plesaunce,
That I was born, allas, what me is wo,
That day of us mot make desseveraunce!
For tyme it is to ryse and hennes go,
Or ellis I am lost for evere-mo!
O nyght, alias! why nyltow over us hove,
As longe as whan Almena lay by Jove?

'O blake nyght, as folk in bokes rede,
That shapen art by God this world to hyde

81

At certeyn tymes wyth thi derke wede,
That under that men myghte in reste abide,
Wel oughten bestes pleyne, and folk the chide,
That there as day wyth labour wolde us breste,
That thow thus fleest, and deynest us nought reste.

'Thow dost, allas! to shortly thyn offyce,
Thow rakel nyght, ther God, maker of kynde,
The, for thyn haste and thyn unkynde vyce,
So faste ay to oure hemi-sperie bynde,
That nevere more under the ground thou wynde
For now, for thou so hyest out of Troye,
Have I forgon thus hastily my joye!'

This Troilus, that with tho wordes felte,
As thoughte him tho, for piëtous distresse,
The blody teris from his herte melte,
As he that nevere yet swich hevynesse
Assayed hadde, out of so gret gladnesse,
Gan therwithal Criseyde, his lady dere,
In armes streyne, and seyde in this manere:

'O cruel day, accusour of the joye
That nyght and love han stole and faste y-wryen,
A-cursed be thi comyng into Troye,
For every bore hath oon of thi bryghte yën!
Envyous day, what list thee so to spien?
What hastow lost, why sekestow this place,
Ther God thi light so quenche, for his grace?

'Allas! what have thise loveris thee agilt,
Dispitous day? Thyn be the peyne of helle!

For many a lovere hastow slayn, and wilt;
Thy pourynge in wol nowher lat hem dwelle.
What profrestow thi lyght here for to selle?
Go selle it hem that smale selys grave;
We wol the nought, us nedeth no day have.'

And eek the sonne Tytan, gan he chyde,
And seyde, 'O fool, wel may men thee dispyse,
That hast the dawying al nyght by thi syde,
And suffrest hir so soone up fro thee rise,
For to disese loveris in this wyse.
What! holde youre bed ther, thow, and ek thi Morwe!
I bidde God, so yeve yow bothe sorwe.'

Therwith ful sore he syghte, and thus he seyde:
'My lady right, and of my wele or wo
The welle and roote, O goodly myn, Criseyde,
And shal I ryse, alias, and shal I so?
Now fele I that myn herte moot a-two.
For how sholde I my lyf an houre save,
Syn that with yow is al the lyf ich have?

'What shal I doon? For, certes, I not how,
Ne whan, allas! I shal the tyme see
That in this plyt I may ben eft with yow.
And of my lyf, God woot how that shal be,
Syn that desyr right now so byteth me,
That I am deed anoon, but I retourne.
How sholde I longe, allas, fro yow sojourne?

'But natheles, myn owen lady bright,
Yit were it so that I wiste outrely

That I, youre humble servaunt and youre knyght,
Were in your herte set so fermely
As ye in myn, the which thyng, trewely,
Me levere were than thise worldes tweyne,
Yet sholde I bet enduren al my peyne.'

To that Criseyde answerde right anoon,
And with a syk she seyde, 'O herte deere,
The game, y-wys, so ferforth now is goon,
That first shal Phebus fallen fro his spere,
And everich egle been the dowves fere,
And every roche out of his place sterte,
Er Troilus out of Criseydes herte.

GLOSSARY.—*Hove*: abide. *Breste*: afflict. *Bore;* hole. *Outrely*: utterly. *Me levere*: I would rather.

Chaucer, when he wrote of love, had that 'sublimity in tender-ness' that Swinburne, with truth, said was the reason of Word-worth's genius at its highest. Chaucer had also the sublimity in sweetness which Wordsworth had not, and which is one of the rarest of qualities. Yet, although Chaucer had all the lightness and brightness of a fiery spirit, as Swinburne said of Nashe, he has not, like Wordsworth, seen the Burning Bush.

Indeed, Chaucer's was a different sublimity and a different ten-derness from that of Wordsworth. The sublimity and tenderness of Wordsworth were those of a man who had learned godship, who had worked that he might attain it,—teaching and healing with wise and soothing words his little child the dust. The sublim-ity and tenderness of Chaucer, whose love-poems are among the most noble, most gentle, most moving, and most honey-sweet of our language, neither teach nor heal. They are not those of a god who had once been a man, they are those of a gentle giant who has retained all his humanity and whose preferred companions are men. If he writes of the poor, he has the sweet compassion of the warm human giant for the little, the cold, the hungry. But when Villon writes of hunger, of cold, he is in the centre of the tragedy;—it is not a case of compassion: he too has been destitute, naked,' dénué' as the worm, cold as the skeleton, with that chill which is brought about by starvation and want:

Derechef je laisse en pitié
À trois petits enfants tous nus
Nommés en ce présent traitié,
Pauvres orphelins impervus,
Tous déchauffés, tous dépourvus,
Et dénués comme le ver,
J'ordonne qu'ils soient pourvus
Au moins pour passer cet hiver.

Premièrement Colin Laurent,
Gérard Gossouin, et Jean Marceau,
Dépourvus de bien, de parents,
Qui n'ont vaillant l'anse d'un seau,
Chacun de mes biens, un faisceau,
Ou quatre blancs, s'ils aiment mieux:
Ils mangeront maint bon morceau,
Les enfants, quand ils seront vieux.

* * *

Item, je laisse aux hospitaux
Mes chassis tissus d'araignée;

Et aux gisants sous les étaux,
Chacun sur œil une grognée:
Trembler à chére refrognée,
Maigres, velus et morfondus,
Chausses courtes, robe rognée,
Gelés, meurtris et enfondus.

GLOSSARY.—*Derechef:* again. *Traitié:* agreement. *Dépourvus:* destitute. *Qui n'ont vaillant l'anse d'un seau:* (proverb) possessing nothing. *Chassis:* folding bedstead. *Tissus d'araignée:* with bedclothes made out of a spider's web. *Grognée:* blow. *Trembler à chére refrognée:* I bequeath them the shiver brought about by starvation and want. *Velus:* shaggy. *Morfondus:* chilled and wasted. *Chausses:* stockings. *Rognée:* cut short, pared, eaten away. *Enfondus* (a Poictevan word): drenched through by the rain.

Villon was a companion of Tom Rynosseros. He is a poet of the thick Cimmerian darkness, the smoke and fume of which, however, is spread by flame, arises from real heat and fire.

But Chaucer—and this is true, also, of the lesser English and Scottish poets of his time (see the Note on John Gower, page 79)—is a poet of light. It is interesting to compare the peculiar shining quality of Chaucer with the lucency of Marlowe. The former glitters, like dew upon a forest under the sun. The latter has a still, bright lucency like that upon still water, or a 'faint eternal eventide of gems'.

Chaucer knew nothing of the black powers that rule the world, or the dark places of the heart. It was to the sweet things of the earth, and 'the blisful light,' to an earthy god of growing things, that this gentle giant knelt 'with dredful hart and glad devocioun'.

XXIV

Notes on Certain Poems by Dunbar, Skelton, Gower, and a Poem by An Anonymous Poet

'Poets', Swinburne said in his *Miscellanies*, may be divided into two exhaustive but not exclusive classes,—the gods of harmony and creation, the giants of energy and invention.'

If this be so, Dunbar, Dryden, and Whitman are the ungodlike giants of our poetry.

The sounds arising from these Titans vary from the hot, earthy sound, the rumbling noise of volcanoes about to burst into flames, of Dryden, to the sonorous and oceanic harmony of certain of Whitman's greatest poems,—or the sound of the huge thundering footsteps of that Blind Harry, William Dunbar.

Sometimes Dunbar is a blinded, blundering, earthy giant, sometimes he has the vastness and strength of a genial, blustering, boisterous north wind,—a geniality that can blacken and turn dangerous. Yet even when he is most wind-like, his spirit has at the same time a queerly animal quality,—almost a smell; his genius has a terrible animal force, stinking and rank like that of Swift; but it is for the most part a genial and friendly rankness, unlike that of Swift. This rank darkness and animal stink is present, or can be present, in nearly all genius, but in most, 'the angel that stands near the naked man' has interfused it with sweetness and light.

Dryden, to return to him for a moment, is a Cyclops, a giant with one red eye; he is formed of thick earth and of raging fire, but light, apart from the light that comes from that fire, that huge forge of earthy things, is not for him.

But here comes the sound of the tempestuous voice, the huge thundering footsteps of Blind Harry:

> Harry, Harry, hobillschowe!
> Se quha is cummyn nowe,
> Bot I wait nevir howe
> With the quhorle wynd?
> A soldane owt of Seriand land,
> A gyand strang for to stand,
> That with the strenth of my hand
> Beres may bynd.
>
> Yet I trowe that I vary,
> I am the nakit Blynd Hary,
> That lang has bene in the Fary
> Farleis to fynd;
> And yit gif this be nocht I,
> I wait I am the spreit of Gy;
> Or elkis go by the sky
> Licht as the lynd.

*   *   *

Quha is cummyn heir, bot I,
A bauld bustuous bellamy,
At your Corss to mak a cry,
    With a hie sowne.
Quhilk generit am of gyandes kynd,
Fra strang Hercules be strynd;
Of all the occident of Ynd,
    My eldaris bair the crowne.

My fore grantschir, hecht Fyn MacKnowle,
That dang the devill and gart him yowle,
The skyis rangd quhen he wald scowle,
    And trublit all the air:
He got my grantschir Gog Magog;
Ay quhen he dansit, the warld wald schog,
Five thousand ellis yeid in his frog
    Of Heiland pladdis, and mair.

Yet he was bot of tendir youth;
Bot eftir he grewe mekle at fouth
Ellevyne myle wyde was his mouth,
    His teith was ten myle squwair.
He wald upon his tais stand,
And tak the sternis downe with his hand,
And set them in a gold garland
    Above his wyfis hair.

He had a wyf was lang of clift;
Hir hed wan hier than the lift;
The hevyne rerdit quhen scho wold rift;
    The lass was no thing sklendir:
Scho spittit Loch Lomond with her lippis,

Thunner and fyre-flaucht flewe fra her hippis;
Quhen scho was crabit, the son tholit clippis;
The fende durst nocht offend hir.

For cald scho tuke the fever tertane;
For all the claith of Fraunce and Bertane,
Wald nocht be till her leg a gartane,
Thocht scho was ying and tender;

* * *

My father, mekle Gow Mackmorne,
Out of that wyfis wame was schorne,
For litilness scho was forlorne,
     Sic a kempe to beir:
Or he of eld was yeris thre',
He wald step our the Oceane fe',
The Mone sprang never above his kne;
     The hevyn had of him feir.

One thousand yere is past fra mynd
Sen I was generit of his kynd,
Full far among the deserts of Ynde,
     Amang lyoun and beir:
Baith the King Arthour and Gawaine
And mony bauld berne in Brettane,
Ar deid, and in the weris slane,
     Sen I couth weild a speir.

* * *

GLOSSARY.—*Farleis*: wonders (?). *Bustuous*: boisterous. *Bellamy*: boon companion. *Strynd*: race, offspring, kindred. *Dang*: knocked out, struck. *Yowle*: scream, howl. *Schog*: shake. *Yeid*: went. *Frog*: coat. *Fouth*: abundance. *Tais*: toes. *Lift*: firmament. *Rift*: belch. *Fyre-flaucht*: lightning, wild-fire. *Crabit*: peevish, crabbed. *Berne*: man. *Weris*: wars.

As we have already seen in the Note on Texture (page 19), consonants are organically ingrown with the vowels: consonants 'determine the specific nature of the latter's manifestment'.

'In the deepest tones of harmony.' wrote Schopenhauer, quoted by Wagner in his book on Beethoven, 'in the fundamental bass-notes, I recognise the lowest degree of the objectivation of the Will, inorganic nature, the mass of the planet. All the higher tones … are to be regarded … as the accessory vibrations of the deep fundamental tone, at the sound of which they are always to be heard softly vibrating. … This is analogous to the view which requires that all bodies and organisations of nature shall be taken as arising in course of gradual evolution from the mass of the planet: this development is their support as well as their source. … Thus the ground bass is to us in harmony, as inorganic nature is to the world, the rudest mass upon which everything rests, and from which everything rises and is developed.'

If we apply, as we may do, the above to poetry, we may substitute consonants for the bass-notes, vowels for the higher tones.

Now, it would be impossible to say that the higher tones, the vowels, of the terrific Blind Harry, 'can be heard softly vibrating'. But certainly the huge consonantal system is 'the rude mass of the planet', only endowed with a gigantic Will.

*   *   *

Dunbar's other poems are roared out by a genial, blustering

boisterous north wind, caring nothing for smoothness,—invigorating, not appeasing. Sometimes the roughness dies down, and the sound is like that of a stilled cold wind blowing in the branches of a tree heavy with leaves, creaking discordantly in the tree's veins.

Both the girl in Dunbar's 'Ane Brash of Wowing' and the girl of Skelton's 'Lullay, lullay' are strayed from Fairyland—but how different is the untamed rough vigour of the first from that strange lullaby, blown by a stilled wind out of a cold fairyland beyond our sight,—the fairyland out of which, one day, will drift 'La Belle Dame sans Merci'.

Dunbar's is a fairyland inhabited by the kind of fairies that colts and calves might see,—and from that land, the cuckoo, the woodgrouse, have flown, bringing back a 'rubye appil' from the same tree from which Eve had plucked an apple for Adam.

Everything is vaster than real life. The woman in 'Ane Brash of Wowing' and the strange lout she is wooing, are giants. He is the naked Blind Harry as he was in youth.

Sometimes the consonants used are slightly rough or hairy, the words have a kind of coltish roughness and un-couthness of surface and movement, and the vowel-sounds change from a cold tunelessness, sharp as the sound of a wind creaking in a tree, to a piercing, harsh, high, inhuman curlew cry, as in

> … My clype, my unspaynit jyane

and

> Fow leis me that graceles gane,

which is very strange, contrasted with the wooden clapping sound brought about by the dulled yet hard consonants of 'clype' and 'gane', and the later 'claver' and 'curldodie',—and the dulled, closing-in vowels of the following passage:

> Quod he, my claver, and my curldodie,
> My hony soppis, my sweit possodie,

*   *   *

> Ye brek my hairt, my bony ane!

ANE BRASH OF WOWING

> In secreit place this hyndir nycht
> I hard ane beyrne say till ane bricht,
> My hunny, my hairt, my houp, my heill,
> I haif bene lang your lufar leill,
>   And can of yow gett confort nane;
> How lang will ye with denger deill?
>   Ye brek my hairt, my bony ane.

*   *   *

> 'Te he' quod scho, and gaif ane gowf,
> Be still my tuchan and my calfe,
> My new-spain'd howphyn fra the sowk;
> And all the blithnes of my bowk;
> My sweit swankyng, saif yow allane
> Na leid I luiffit all this owk;
>   Fow leis me that graceles gane.

> Quod he, my claver, and my curldodie,
> My hony soppis, my sweit possoddie,
> By nocht oure bosteous to your billie,
> Be warme hartit and nocht illwillie;

* * *

Ye brek my hairt, my bony ane.

Quod scho, my clype, my unspaynit jyane,
With muderis milk yit in your michane,
My belly huddroun, my sweit hurle bawsy,
My huney gukkis, my slawsy gawsy,
    Your musing wald perss ane hairt of stane;
So tak gud confort, my gritheidit slawsy;
    Fow leis me that graceles gane.

Quoth he, my kid, my capirculyoun,
My tender gyrle, my wally gowdy,
My tirly mirly, my crowdy mowdy;

* * *

Ye brek my hairt, my bony ane.

Quoth scho, Now tak me by the hand,
Wylcum, my golk of maryland,
My chirry and my maikles mynyeoun,
My sowker sweit as ony unyeoun,
    My strummil stirk, yit new to spane,
I am applyid to your opinyoun;
    Fow leis me that graceles gane.

He gaif til hir ane appill ruby;
Grammercy! quod scho, my sweit cowhuby.

* * *

Fow leis me that graceles gane.

94

GLOSSARY.—*Hyndir*: last. *Beyrne*: youth. *Ane bricht*: a fair one. *Hunny*: honey. *Houp*: hope. *Heill*: welfare. *Lufar*: lover. *Denger*: disdain. *Howphyn*: dolt. *Bowk*: body. *Curldodie*: ribwort plantain. *Clype*: colt. *Gukkis*: fool. *Golk;* cuckoo. *Maryland*: fairyland. *Chirry*: cherry. *Sowker*: sugar. *Strummil*: stumbling. *Stirk*: Ox. *Spane*: wean. *Cowhuby*: cowherd, or booby. *Gane*: face.

John Skelton's 'Lullay, lullay' is one of the most drowsy-sounding poems in our language:

> With Lullay, lullay, like a chylde,
> Thou slepyst to long, thou art begylde.
>
> My darlyng dere, my daysy floure,
>   Let me, quod he, ly in your lap.
>
> Ly styll, quod she, my paramoure,
>   Ly styll hardely, and take a nap.
>   Hys hed was hevy, such was his hap,
> All drowsy dremyng, dround in slepe,
> That of his loue he toke no kepe,
>   With hey, lullay.
>
> With ba, ba, ba, and bas, bas, bas,
>   She cheryshed hym both cheke and chyn,
> That he wyst never wher he was;
>   He had forgoten all dedely syn.
>   He wantyd wyt her love to win.
> He trusted her payment, and lost all hys pray:
> She left hym slepyng, and stole away,
>   With hey, lullay.
>
> The rivers rowth, the waters wan;
>   She sparyd not to wete her fete;

She wadyd over, she found a man
> That halysed her hartely and kyst her swete:
> Thus after her cold she caught a hete.
My lefe, she sayd, rowtyth in hys bed;
I wys he hath an hevy hed
> With hey, lullay.

What dremyst thou, drunckard, drowsy pate!
> Thy lust and lykyng is from thee gone;
Thou blynkerd blowboll, thow wakyst to late,
> Behold, thou lyeste, luggard, alone.
> Well may thou sygh, well may thou grone,
To dele with her so cowardly;
I wys, powle hachet, she bleryd thyne eye.
> With hey, lullay.

The sleepy movement owes much to the drone-sound of the alliteration. I know no poem to equal it for drowsiness, excepting the lines about the House of Sleep in John Gower's 'Ceix and Alcyone' (and of this I will speak later) and the even earlier (fourteenth century) anonymous 'Maid of the Mor',[1] which might have been the song of a wandering bee on some sleepy afternoon. It has, indeed, the circling, wandering, returning movements of the bee:

> Maiden in the mor lay,
> > In the mor lay,
> Seuenyst fulle, seuenist fulle,
> Maiden in the mor lay,
> > In the mor lay

---

[1] *Fourteenth Century Verse and Prose*, edited by Kenneth Sisam, Clarendon Press.

Seuenistes fulle ant a day.

Welle was hire mete;
    Wat was hire mete?
    The primerole ant the,—
The primerole ant the,—
Welle was hire mete;
Wat was hire mete?
    The primerole ant the violet.

Welle (was hire dryng);
    Wat was hire dryng?
The chelde water of (the) welle-spring.

Welle was hire bour;
    Wat was hire bour?
The rede rose ant te lilie flour.

GLOSSARY.—*Mor*: moor. *Seuenyst*: seven nights. *Hire*: her. *Mete*: meat. *Primerole*: primrose. *Dryng*: drink. *Chelde*: chilled.

This really is a miracle of poetry, with the change in the vowel sounds of the alliteration,—the darkening from 'maiden' to 'mor' and the lightening again to the non-alliterative but assonantal 'lay',—the change in the second verse from 'welle' to 'wat',—(this latter having less an effect of darkening than of wandering).

The sound produces a strange effect of moving further away at the end of each line,—(not dying away exactly),—and then of returning with the beginning of the next line. Perhaps this is because the accent falls on the first syllable in many of the lines.

The slight change in speed—(I use this word for want of a

97

better one, since it is a sleepy poem, and yet slowness is not the word either)—is due to the pause between the echoes of

> Maiden in the m̄or lay,
> In the m̄or lay

—(where the accent, in the two lines, is changed), crossed by the line

> Seuenyst fulle, seuenist fulle

—which is faintly quicker, because of the three-syllabled 'seuenyst'.

* * *

Dionysius the Areopagite, speaking on the Divine Names, said: 'All things in motion desire to make known their own proper movement, and this is an aspiration after the Divine Peace of the whole, which, unfailing, preserves all things from falling, and, unmoved, guards the idiosyncrasy and life of all moving things, so that the things moved, being at peace among themselves, perform their own proper functions'.

John Gower lived but in the light of a mortal day; but Poetry is only another of the Divine Names, and each poet, even if his day is but mortal, is part of the great light. Gower did, though neither a seraph nor an archangel nor a giant, make known the proper movement of his theme,—as in the sleepy sound of these lines from 'Ceix and Alcyone':

> This Iris, fro the hihe stage
> Which undertake hath the message
> Hire reyny cope dede upon,
> The which was wonderlie begone
> With colours of diverse hewe,

98

An hundred mo than men it knewe;
The hevene lich into a bowe
Sche bende, and as sche cam down lowe,
The God of Slep when that sche fond;
And that was in a strange lond,
Which marcheth upon Chymerie:
For ther, as seith the Poesie,
The God of Slep hath mad his hous,
Which of entaille is merveilous.

      Under an hell there is a cave,
Which of the sonne mai naught have.
So that noman mai knowe ariht
The point between the dai and nyht:
Ther is no fyr, ther is no sparke,
Ther is no dore, which mai charke,
Whereof an ihye scholde unschette,
So that inward ther is no lette.
And for to speke of that withoute,
Ther stan no gret tree nyh aboute
Wher on ther myhte crowe or pie
Alihte, for to clepe or crie;
Ther is no cok to crowe day,
No beste non which noise may;
The hell bot al aboute round
Ther is gravende upon the ground
Popi, which beith the sed of slep,
With other herbes suche an hep.
A stille water for the nones
Rennende upon the smale stones,
Which hihte of Lethe's the rivere,
Under that hell is such manere

Ther is, which gifth gret appetit
To slepe. And thus full of delit
Slep hath his hous; and of his couch
Withinne his chambre if I schal touche,
Of hebenus that slepi tree
The bordes al aboute be.

GLOSSARY.—*Hihe*: high. *Hire*: her. *Reyny*: rainy. *Lich*: light. *Sche*:
she. *Hell*: hall. *Charke*: shut loudly. *Ihye*: eye. *Unschette*: unshut. *Lette*:
prevention. *Gravende*: growing. *Rennende*: running. *Hihte*: called,
named. *Hebenus*: ebony.

The sleepy sound owes much to the rarity of pauses.

In other poems of Gower's, the shining, glistening quality that
was part of the physical and spiritual nature of Chaucer's poetry
was present, too, in his contemporary, Gower, though Gower's
day was not universal, like Chaucer's, nor was he living in the
midst of that day; it was, with him, a lovely memory of youth,—
the memory of one hot morning when, like the Orfeo of a still
earlier poet,

He might se him bisides
    Oft in hot undertides,
The king o' fairy, with his rout
Com to hunt him al about
With dim cri and bloweing
    And houndes also with him berking.

For Gower it was *one* day, never to be lived again, not all days:

The Flees he tok and goth to Bote,
The Sonne schyneth bryhte and hote,

100

The Flees of Gold schon forth withal,
The water glistreth overal.
      Medea wepte and sigheth ofte,
And stod upon a Tour aloft:
And prively withinne hirselfe,
Ther here it nouther ten, ne twelve,
      Sche preide, and seide 'O God him spede,
      The kniht which hath my maidenheide.'
And ay sche loketh toward thyle,
But whan sche sih withinne a while
The Flees glistrende ayein the Sonne,
Sche saide 'Ha lord, now al is wonne,
Hir kniht the field hath overcome;
Hir lord, that he ne were alonde,
Bot I dar take this on honde,
If that sche hadde wynges two,
Sche wolde have flowe with him tho
Strawht ther he was in the Bot.

GLOSSARY.—*Ther here it nouther ten, ne twelve*: in other words, she did not heed the passing of time. *Thyle*: the isle. *Alonde*: on the land.

We were to see that sun of youth again, shining like the Golden Fleece, four hundred years later, in certain poems of William Morris.

But to return to John Skelton. Certain of his poems to young girls have the notes we hear in the woods in spring, wild bird-songs, a murmuration of starlings, a watch of nightingales, and a charm of goldfinches. Sometimes they grow sharp as a spring flower, and from the same ground from which sprang this refrain of an Elizabethan song by an anonymous author, rediscovered by Mr. Norman Ault:

With lily, germander and sops-in-wine,
With sweet-briar
And bonfire
And strawberry wire
And columbine.

* * *

Never, for a moment, is there heard the voice of a man.

In the lovely 'To Maystres Isabell Pennell', after the first three lines, each line is the shape of a honeycomb.

'In the construction', says Mr. Tickner Edwardes in his book on the honey-bee (Methuen), 'of the six-sided cell, with its base composed of three rhombs or diamonds, the bee has adapted a form which our greatest arithmeticians admit to be the best possible for her requirements, and she endeavours to keep to this form whenever practicable.'

Here, then, is the six-sided cell, with its base composed of six rhombs or diamonds:

My mayden Isabell,
Reflaring rosabell,
The flagrant camamell;
The ruddy rosary,
The soverayne rosemary,
The praty strawbery;

* * *

and the 'endeless welth' of which we hear at the end of the poem, is that which the dusky workers in fields and gardens

102

bring home to their hives when they

> ... having laboured hard from light to light
> With golden thighes come singing home at night;

and like John Day's bee,

> The windowes of my hive, with blossoms dight,
> Are porters to let in our comfort, light.

'To Maystres Isabell Pennell', as Mr. de la Mare has said in *Come Hither*, is 'the loveliest and gayest song of praise and sweetness to "a young thing" I have ever seen.'

> By saynt Mary, my lady,
> > Your mammy and your dady
> Brought forth a godely babi!
>
> > My mayden Isabell,
> Reflaring rosabell,
> The flagrant camamell;
>
> > The ruddy rosary,
> The soverayne rosemary,
> The praty strawbery;
>
> > The columbyne, the nepte,
> The ieloffer well set,
> The propre vyolet;
>
> > Enuwyd your colowre
> Is lyke the dasy flowre
> After the Aprill showre;
>
> > Sterre of the morrow gray,
> The blossom on the spray,

The fresshest flowre of May;

Maydenly demure,
Of womanhode the lure;
Wherfore I make you sure,

It were an hevenly helth,
It were an endeles welth,
A lyfe for God hymselfe,

To here this nightingale,
Amonge the byrdes smale,
Warbelynge in the vale,

Dug, dug,
lug, iug,
Good yere and good luk,
With chuk, chuk, chuk, chuk!

In the twist of this poem we have the spring bird's song, and the closely juxtaposed assonances 'May' and 'Maydenly demure' are round like buds.

'Ieloffer', says Mr. de la Mare in a note upon this poem in *Come Hither*, 'gelofer, gelofre, gillofre, gelevor, gillyvor, gillofer, jerefloure, gerraflour—all these are ways of spelling "gillyflower" "gelofre" coming nearest to its original French: "giroflée", meaning spiced like the clove.[2] There were of old, I find, three kinds of gillyflowers: the clove, the stock, and the wall. It was the first of these kinds that was meant in the earlier writers by the small clove carnation (or Coronation, because it was made into chaplets or garlands). Its Greek name was dianthus (the flower divine); and its

---

[2] 'Gelevor'—a sweet red fire coming after the frost?—E. S.

twin sister is the Pink, so called because its edges are pinked, that is, jagged, notched, scalloped, Country names for it are Sweet John, Pagiants, Blunket, and Sops-in-Wine, for it spices what it floats in, and used to be candied for a sweetmeat. Blossoming in July, the gillyflower suggests July-flower, and if Julia is one's sweetheart, it may also be a Julie-flower. So one name may carry many echoes. It has been truly described as a gimp and gallant flower, and, says Parkington, who wrote *Paradisus Terrestris*, it was the chiefest of account in Tudor gardens. There was a garden in Westminster in his own time belonging to a Master Ralph Tuggie, famous all London over for the beauty and variety of its gillyflowers: *e.g.* "Master Tuggie his Princesse", "Master Bradshaw his daintie Ladie", "The Red Hulo", "The Fair Maid of Kent", "Lustie Gallant", "The Speckled Tawny", and "Ruffling Robin".'

To these enumerated by Mr. de la Mare, I might add these pinks or carnations that once grew in Master Tuggie's garden, and that I have gathered from my brother Sacheverell Sitwell's book, *Old-fashioned Flowers*, 'Master Tuggie his Rose Gillyflower', the 'Striped Tawny', the 'Flaked', and the 'Feathered Tawny', the 'Chrystall' or 'Chrystalline', the 'Red Chrystall', the 'Fragrant' and the 'Striped Savadge'; the 'Rose Savadge', the 'Greatest Granado', the 'Cambersine', the 'Bristol Blush', the 'Red Dover', the 'Queen's Dainty', the 'Brazil', the 'Turkey …', together with Master Parkinson's 'Feathered or Jagged Pinks', 'Star Pinks', and 'Great Thrifts'—which are called, also, 'Sweet Johns' and 'Sweet Williams'.

The sweet perfume of those pinks remains to us after four centuries. It blows through a later garden:

> To smell those odours that do rise
> From out the wealth and spiceries:

So smels the flowre of blooming Clove,
Or roses smother'd in the stove:
So smels the Aire of spicèd wine;
Or essences of Jessamine:
So smels the breath about the hives,
Where wel the work of hony thrives,
And all the busy Factours come
Laden with wax and hony home:
So smell those neat and woven Bowers
All over-archt with Oringe flowers,
And almond blossoms, that so mix
To make rich those Aromatikes.
So smell those bracelets and those bands
Of Amber chaft between the hands,
When thus embalmed they transpire
A noble perfume from the fire.

*   *   *

Though here, the perfume is more spiced, and the air in which it lives, less cool.

XXV

Notes on Herrick

The spirit of Herrick might have been the 'apparition' seen Anno 1670, near Cirencester, of whom John Aubrey tells us in his *Miscellanies*: 'Being demanded whether a good spirit or a bad, returned no answer, but disappeared with a curious perfume and a most melodious Twang. Mr. W. Lilly believes it was a Fairie.'

Or again, he could have appeared among those spirits that Mr. Thomas Allen, 'in those darke (Elizabethan) times Astrologer, Mathematician, and Conjurer', met 'coming up his stairs like bees' (John Aubrey, *Brief Lives*). At other times his spirit resembles those small birds which, according to Antonio Galvano of New Spain,' live of the dew, and the juyce of flowers and roses. Their feathers bee small and of divers colours. They be greatly esteemed to work gold with. They die or sleepe every yeare in the moneth of October, sitting upon a little bough in a warme and close place. They revive or wake againe in the moneth of April after the flowers be sprung.'

* * *

The poems are as subtle, and as delicate, as the warm airs that awaken those little birds 'whose feathers be greatly esteemed to work gold with',—they are faint as the breaths of air and perfume wafting through the branches of the flowering plum, or the stillness of a sweet night.

> The night is still,
> The darkness knows
> How far away
> A wavering rill
> Of darkness goes;
> Though no bough hums,
> Between April and May
> A streak of plum-blossom comes.

But that exquisite fragment is from a song by Gordon Bottomley, not by Herrick.

In the flawlessly beautiful 'Lovers how they come and part', the only emphasis is in the shapes of the pear and plum, the only colour that which steals into them:

> A Gyges Ring they beare about them still,
> To be, and not seen when and where they will.
> They tread on clouds, and though they sometimes fall,
> They fall like dew, but make no noise at all.
> So silently they one to th' other come,
> As colours steale into the Peare or Plum,
> And Aire-like, leave no pression to be seen
> Where e'er they met, or parting place has been.

To these shapes the *p*'s give body,—the first shape being longer

108

and more delicate, tapering down from the roundness, through the long double vowels, to the fading r,—the second rounder, and with more body, because of the enclosing *pl* and *m* '… So silently', with the alliterative *s*'s, the rising vowels, give another, but fainter, embodiment, 'clouds' melts into 'come,' 'come' fades into 'colours'. 'Peare or Plum' have the faintest echo in the *p* and the *pl* of 'parting place'. There is the slightest possible lengthening of line,—a lengthening so faint as to be hardly perceptible, that comes from the wavering movement of the double-vowelled 'Peare' and 'Aire' (with that hardly-perceptible flutter caused by the *r*)—and the echo of these in 'where e'er'. 'Beare' has not the same wavering movement, because the *b*, which begins the word, concentrates it.

In these lovely lines from 'Corinna going a-Maying':

> Rise; and put on your Foliage, and be seene
> To come forth, like the Spring-time, fresh and greene;
>> And sweet as *Flora*.   Take no care
>> For Jewels for your Gowne, or Haire:
>> Feare not; the leaves will strew
>> Gemms in abundance upon you,

the leaves strew their gems upon us, in the very sound of those incredibly faint, wavering, dropping movements of 'care' and 'Haire'—(the latter being a little longer in fading than the former)—and in the immaterial fluttering sound of the internal *r*'s in 'Spring', 'greene', 'strew'.

These wavering airs, these faint rills of air that come and go, as with the subtle dropping sound of 'dew' and the wavering sound of 'air' in the poem 'Upon Julia's Haire fill'd with Dew',— the faint sharpening sound of 'dew' softening to the warmer sound of the 'Ju' in 'Julia' and the sound of 'too', the points of light given by the long assonantal *e's* of 'Leaves', 'Beames', 'Streames',—the dewy *l's*,—these subtleties are like the bloom upon the poem, the differences in the glitter of that dew on leaves and hair.

> Dew sate on Julia's haire,
>   And spangled too
> Like Leaves that laden are
>   With trembling Dew:
> Or glitter'd to my sight,
>   As when the Beames
> Have their reflected light
>   Daunc't by the Streames.

In 'The Night-Piece to Julia' there is a firefly-like darting of the movement, due to the fact that the rhyme occurs internally, in the last word but one, in the first, second, and fifth lines of each verse (excepting in the third verse, where the opportunity does not arise, as the last word is a double-syllabled one):

> Her Eyes the Glow-worme lend thee,
> The Shooting Starres attend thee,
>   And the Elves also,
>   Whose little eyes glow,
> Like the sparks of fire, befriend thee.
>
> No Will-o'-th'-Wispe mis-light thee;
> Nor Snake, or Slow-worme bite thee:
>   But on, on thy way
>   Not making a stay,
> Since Ghost ther's none to affright thee.

Let not the darke thee cumber;
What though the Moon do's slumber?
    The Starres of the night
    Will lend thee their light,
Like Tapers cleare without number.

Then Julia let me wooe thee,
Thus, thus to come unto me:
    And when I shall meet
    Thy silv'ry feet,
My soule Ile pour into thee.

Excepting in the third verse, where it does not occur, this internal rhyme gives emphasis, and we have the droning end, in the first two verses, caused by the fact that these lines end, invariably, with the same word, 'thee'.

    Her Eyes the Glow-worme lend thee,
    The Shooting Starres attend thee, [etc.]

The whole movement gives us the feeling of a lady in rustling silks flying down the midnight branch-shadowed paths, followed by the firefly-darting sound caused by the much shorter and quicker internal lines:

    And the Elves also,
    Whose little eyes glow.

The quickness is due to the running movement of 'And the' in the first of these two lines, and 'little' in the second—words much faster than those in the previous lines—words on which no pause is made. So that we understand from the sound that the lady is in a hurry, as she flies across the moonlit grass, for fear of the will-o'-the-wisp, the snake, and the slow-worm—and that all tiny and bright things are darting from the skies and from the dark woods to help her on her way with their sudden and lovely gleaming.

The poem 'Upon Julia's Voice', with the subtlety of the longer rhyme to 'voice' upon 'noise' and the dropping sound from 'chamber' to 'Amber', is largely dependent for beauty on the extremely sweet vowels, enclosed, sometimes, in a most intricate scheme of *s*'s; the only loud sound in the whole poem being produced by the *D* in 'Damned'. In fact, the whole of the verse is built upon a subtle foundation of *s*'s,—there are only three words beginning with hard consonants in the song, and of these, two are almost muted. I know of no poet—not even Milton or Pope, who could manage sibilants better than Herrick. As for the vowel-sounds in this poem, they are as smooth and as un-poignant as the lovely voice the poem is praising:

> So smooth, so sweet, so silv'ry is thy voice,
> As, could they hear, the Damn'd would make no noise,
> But listen to thee, (walking in thy chamber),
> Melting melodious words to Lutes of Amber.

In the first two lines of 'The Weeping Cherry'

> I saw a Cherry weep, and why?
> Why wept it? but for shame,

the alliteration, and the profound vowel-sound in 'weep', prolongs the length of the lines (but almost imperceptibly) and makes them heavier, as though the cherry, and the light and lovely branch from which it sprang, were made heavier by that rich weight of dew:

112

I saw a Cherry weep, and why?
        Why wept it? but for shame,
Because my Julia's lip was by,
        And did out-red the same.
But pretty Fondling, let not fall
        A tear at all for that:
Which Rubies, Corralls, Scarlets, all
        For tincture, wonder at.

And we, too, may wonder at the 'Rubies, Corralls, Scarlets'. But how are we to explain the faint, soft beauty of 'The Primrose'—a poem whose life is as faint as that of the flower, whose perfume is as intangible:

        Aske me why I send you here
This sweet Infanta of the yeere?
        Aske me why I send to you
This Primrose, thus bepearl'd with dew?
        I will whisper to your eares
The sweets of Love are mixt with teares.

        Aske me why this flower do's show
So yellow-green, and sickly too?
        Aske me why the stalk so weak
And bending (yet it doth not break?)
        I will answer, These discover
What fainting hopes are in a Lover.

These songs and sounds, the faint warm rills of air, and draughts of cooler air, these whispers of air, ripples of air, steal on the ear; the primrose-pale, primrose-scented dews of the early morning poems, fleeting and immaterial, are gone in the moment of a dream. There is neither harshness nor pain, nor is there agony in death,—there is scarcely sorrow. ... Only the dew fades on the primrose, the golden beauty of the daffodil.

> ... We die,
>   As your hours doe, and drie
>   Away
>   Like to the Summer's raine;
>   Or as the pearles of Morning's dew,
>   Ne'er to be founde againe.

And that fading is only the reason for a new invocation:

> So when or you or I are made
> A fable, song, or fleeting shade;
> All love, all liking, all delight
> Lies drown'd with us in endless night.
>   Then while time serves, and we are but decaying;
>   Come, my Corinna, come, lets goe a-Maying.

All his funeral songs are only for the passing of a honeybee, dead in the first delicate snows of winter; his bass-notes are like the deep droning sound that comes from a hive. To him, death, and life, and the business of life, were a sweet scent, intangible but rich, like the uncorrupted fame of which he wrote in his epigram 'To His Honoured Kinsman, Sir William Soame';—a fame that

> Casts forth a light like to a Virgin flame,
> And as it shines, it throws a scent about,
> As when a Rain-bow in perfumes goes out.

XXVI

Notes on Smart, With A Note on Gerard Manley Hopkins

To this earth-bound St. Francis, this earth-covered incomplete saint, comforting those who are not irradiated, with the words 'The glory of God is always in the East, but cannot be seen for the Cloud of the Crucifixion', 'all things have become light, never again to set, and the setting has believed in the rising. This is the new Creation.'[1] All things were light come from above: 'For water is not of solid constituents, but is dissolved from precious stones above';—though the Crucifixion was his, amid the deathly cold of Bedlam, his madness was not a darkness but a light. His body knew the lack of bread, and had known the sin of drunkenness, but yet to the end of his life, his soul, his apprehension of the world, were those of Thomas Traherne's child:

---

[1] St. Clement: Address to the Greeks.

Certainly Adam in Paradise had not more sweet and curious apprehensions of the world than I, when I was a child.

* * *

All appeared new, and strange at first, inexpressibly rare and delightful and beautiful. … My knowledge was Divine, I knew by intuition those things which since my Apostasy, I collected, again by the highest reason. My very ignorance was advantageous. I seemed as one brought into the Estate of Innocence. All things were spotless and pure and glorious: yea, and infinitely mine, and joyful and precious. I knew not that there were any sins or complaints or laws. I dreamed not of poverties, contentions, or vices. All tears and quarrels were hidden from mine eyes. Everything was at rest, free and immortal. I knew nothing of sins and death or rents or exaction, either for tribute or bread. In the absence of these I was entertained like an Angel with the works of God in their splendour and glory, I saw all in the peace of Eden: Heaven and earth did sing my Creator's praises, and could not make more melody to Adam, than to me. All Time was Eternity, and a perpetual Sabbath. …

The corn was orient and immortal wheat, which never should be reaped, nor was ever sown. I thought it had stood from everlasting to everlasting. The dust and stones were as precious as gold: the gates were at first the end of the world. The green trees when I saw them first through one of the gates transported and ravished me, their sweetness and unusual beauty made my heart to leap, and almost mad with ecstasy, they were such strange and wonderful things. The men! O what venerable and reverend creatures did the aged seem! Immortal Cherubims! And young men glittering and sparkling Angels, and maids strange seraphic pieces of life and beauty! Boys and girls tumbling in the street, and playing, were moving jewels. I knew not that they were born or should die; But all things abided eternally as they were in their proper places. Eternity was manifest in the Light of the Day, and something infinite behind everything appeared: which talked with my expectation and moved my desire. The city seemed to stand in Eden, or to be built in Heaven. The streets were mine, the temple was mine, the gold and silver were mine, as much as their sparkling eyes, fair skins and ruddy faces. The skies were mine, and so were the sun and moon and stars, and all the world was mine; and I the only spectator and enjoyer of it. I knew no churlish proprieties, nor lands, nor divisions; but all proprieties and divisions were mine: all treasures and the possession of them.

In that great poem, 'A Hymn to David', descending like an angel to the madman of genius, the saint of love, in his earthly prison, all things of clay, all objects of our daily life, were changed into beings formed from the light that is in Heaven. The colours, the light, are deeper, are richer, like

> The topaz blazing like a lamp
> Among the mines beneath

The saint in him pierced down to the essence of all things seen—and that essence was light, with all its variations of warmth, richness, piercingness, glow. It is impossible to know how he produces that quintessence of light. But if, for instance, we take Verse LXV:

> For Adoration, beyond match,
> The scholar bulfinch aims to catch
> The soft flute's ivory touch;

117

And, careless on the hazle spray,
The daring redbreast keeps at bay
The damsel's greedy clutch.

we shall see how in the lovely softening from the *fl* of 'flutes' to
the *i* of 'ivory', the change from the fullness of the one-syllabled
word 'flutes' to the long warm *i* of 'ivory' with the quavering two
syllables that follow, in that word,—the transposition of the *ulf* of
'bulfinch' to the *flu* of 'flutes',—the actual sound seems to echo
the warmth, the very glow, of the scholar bulfinch's and the dar-
ing redbreast's sweet bosoms.

In Verse LII

For Adoration seasons change,
And order, truth, and beauty range,
Adjust, attract, and fill:
The grass the polyanthus cheques:
And polish'd porphyry reflects
　By the descending rill.

Rich almonds colour to the prime
For Adoration; tendrils climb;
　And fruit-trees pledge their gems;
And Ivis with her gorgeous vest
Builds for her eggs her cunning nest,
　And bell-flowers bow their stems.

The colour is so rich as not to be of this world.

And yet, the flowers plucked by Smart are flowers of this
earth, though they are known by the angels, 'worshipping Christ
with the People of the Rose, which is a nation of living
sweetness'.

Blake's lily of the vale was the white and ineffably sweet soul of the lily. Blake's marigold was a flower known to Persephone:

'Art thou a flower? Art thou a nymph? I see thee now a flower,
Now a nymph! I dare not pluck thee from thy dewy bed.'

The Golden Nymph replied, 'Pluck thou my flower, Oothoon
the mild!

Another flower shall spring, because the soul of sweet delight
Can never pass away.' She ceas'd, and clos'd her golden shrine.
Then Oothoon pluck'd the flower, saying: 'I pluck thee from thy
bed,
Sweet flower, and put thee here to glow between my breasts;
And thus I turn my face to where my whole soul seeks.'

Over the waves she went in wing'd exulting swift delight.

*   *   *

A beautiful though perhaps less great poet than Smart, Gerard
Manley Hopkins, (less great because he was not visited directly by
angels of the heavenly fire and light), had, in an almost equal
degree, this acute and strange visual sense, piercing, as I said
above, to the essence of the thing seen. Hopkins, unlike Smart,
heightened the truth, the essence, by endowing them with attri-
butes which at first seem alien, with colours that are sharper,
clearer, more piercing than those that are seen by the common
eye.

This acute and piercing visual apprehension, this sharpening,
and concentration into essence by the means of which I have
spoken, may be found in these lovely lines from 'The May
Magnificat':

Ask of her, the mighty mother:
Her reply puts this other
Question: What is Spring?
Growth in everything—

Flesh and fleece, fur and feather,
Grass and greenworld all together.
Star-eyed strawberry-breasted
Throstle above her nested

Cluster of bugle blue eggs thin
Forms and warms the life within;
And bird and blossom swell
In sod or sheath or shell.

* * *

When drop-of-blood-and-foam-dapple
Bloom lights the orchard-apple
And thicket and thorp are merry
With silver surfèd cherry

And azuring-over greybell makes
Wood banks and brakes wash wet like lakes
And magic cuckoocall
Caps, clears, and clinches all.

This ecstasy all through mothering earth
Tells Mary her mirth till Christ's birth
To remember and exultation
In God who was her salvation.

In the sharply-seen image of the star-eyed strawberry-breasted thrush, Hopkins says 'strawberry-breasted' because of the freckles on her breast. In the enhanced and deepened colour of the bugle-blue eggs, the sharp *u* of 'bugle' melting into the softer *u* of 'blue' gives the reflection of one in the other, the sisterhood of the deep blue heaven, the flower, and the egg, their colours changing and shifting in the clear light.

The same piercing truth-finding vision produced for us the fair hair of the country youth in this lovely fragment:

> The furl of fresh-leaved dog-rose down
> His cheeks the forth-and-flaunting sun
> Had swarthed about with lion-brown
> Before the Spring was done.
>
> His locks like all a ravel-rope's-end
> With hempen strands in spray—
> Fallow, foam-fallow, hanks—fall'n off their ranks
> Swung down at a disarray.
>
> Or like a juicy and jostling shock
> Of bluebells sheaved in May
> Or wind-long fleeces on the flock
> A day off shearing-day.
>
> Then over his turnèd temples—here—
> Was a rose, or, failing that,
> Rough-Robin or five-lipped campion clear
> For a beauty-bow to his hat,
> And the sunlight sidled, like dewdrops,
>   like dandled diamonds,
> Through the sieve of the straw of his hat.

In this lovely fragment, the comparison of the youth's fair hair with a sheaf of bluebells gives, to me, the fairness of the hair, and shows the straightness of it, the way in which it flaps,—for, of all flowers, only a sheaf of bluebells has this particular limpness.

Here we have a youth, in the midst of his walk, suddenly leaping into the air and dancing for a step or two, because of the fun of being alive on this lovely morning of the late spring. The innocent and sweet movement of this very beautiful fragment is due, partly, to the skilful interposition of an extra syllable from time to time, and an occasional rare extra rhyme; and the clearness and poignant colours of the morning are conveyed by the sounds of 'juicy', 'bluebells', and 'sheaved', with their varying degrees of deep and piercing colour.

We find the same heightening and concentration again, in these beautiful lines about the skies on a May night:

For how to the heart's cheering
The down-dugged ground-hugged grey
Hovers off, the jay-blue heavens appearing
    Of pied and peeled May!
Blue-beating and hoary glow-height; or night, still higher,
With belled fire and the moth-soft Milky Way,
What by your measure is the heaven of desire,
The treasure never eyesight got, nor was ever guessed what for
    the hearing?

A lovely movement, a sense that all is well, that all Creation is part of a controlled and gigantic design, is given by the internal rhymes and assonances,—the movement being like that of a bird flying through the bright air, swooping downward to its nest, then up again through the holy and peaceful light.

XXVII

Notes on Wordsworth

'Three kinds of men', said Eckhart in *Sermons and Collations,* 'see God. The first see Him in faith; they know no more of Him than they can make out through a partition. The second behold God in the light of grace but only as the answer to their longings, as giving them sweetness, devotion, inwardness, and other such-like things which are issuing from His gift. The third kind see Him in the divine light.'

Of these three kinds of men, George Herbert belongs to the second category, Smart and the yet more irradiated Blake to the third. Wordsworth belongs to neither kind, for although to Blake 'even Wordsworth seemed a kind of atheist, who mistook the changing signs of vegetable nature for the unchanging realities of imagination' (Arthur Symons), he was wrong. Wordsworth did not see God through a partition—even one which is of living matter and not made by the hands of men from bricks and dead sticks: to him, 'the lights of faith and of nature are subordinate John Baptists'. He was, indeed, more of the nature of the disciples than, like Shelley, an order of being like the archangels.

The difference between Wordsworth, and Blake, Smart, and their brother in prose, Traherne, is the difference in nature between certain men of God—(difference, not separation).

'It is written.' said St. Bernard,[1] 'the angel who spoke in me.

'And yet there is a difference even here. The angel is in us suggesting what is good, not bestowing it: stimulating us to goodness, not creating goodness. God is so in us as to give the grace, and infuse it into us; or rather, so in us that He Himself is infused and partaken of, so that one need not fear to say that He is one with our substance. For you know "He that is joined unto God is one spirit". The Angel, therefore, is with the soul; God is in the soul. The Angel is in the soul as a comrade, God as life.'

'I am a companion of angels', wrote Blake to his friend Hayley. But these were the companions of his earthly side. He had deeper, more terrible communions than these.

It is the comrade, the angel, that Wordsworth knew on the levels of his life. Though there were days, those moments which contain eternity, when he saw the Burning Bush.

On the levels of his life, he knew light, but it was the light of Reason rather than the innermost secret Flame. He brought to his poetry all the 'household stuffe of Heaven on earth'. And it is a poetry more of the reason than the intellect … a reason which is Life. It is that reason of which St. Augustine spoke when he said, 'The earth was made; but, the earth itself which was made is not life. In the Wisdom of God, however, there is spiritually a certain Reason after which the earth was made. This is life.'

---

[1] On consideration.

124

Reason and Tranquillity were the companion Angels of Wordsworth, as he walked through an everyday world made splendid by the light of a genius which illuminated but did not transform. Common speech and common experience were here, but all made radiant and unforgettable by inspiration. There were days—the *Intimations of Immortality from Recollections of Early Childhood* was such an undying day—when the Pentecostal Flames came, for a moment, to our common speech. The ordinary objects of life became supernatural. The common celandine was still the common celandine, but it was also a star. For Wordsworth had the warmth of the earth and of the human heart, and that genius which was rather of the heart than of the soul had taken all the chill from Reason, till Reason had the pulse of a human, yet a holy, heart.

For his poems are ineffably holy:

> The earth, and every common sight,
> To me did seem
> Apparelled in celestial light.

In the note to that ode which was the mountain on which he and his angels spoke with God (the *Intimations of Immortality from Recollections of Early Childhood*), he says, speaking of his early years: 'I was often unable to think of external things as having external existence, and I communed with all that I saw as something not apart from, but inherent in, my own immaterial nature. Many times while going to school have I grasped at a wall or tree to recall myself from this abyss of idealism to the reality.'

The kernel of all his poems—even when we have to cut to that kernel through an unnecessary husk furred with earth, have a singular purity and fidelity. Matthew Arnold said of him, 'It might seem that Nature not only gave him the matter for his poem, but wrote his poem for him'. That fine critic Arthur Symons, quoting this, adds, 'He has none of the poet's pride in his own invention, only a confidence in the voices that he has heard speaking when others were aware of nothing but silence. Thus it is that in the interpretation of natural things he can be absolutely pellucid, like pure light, which reveals to us every object in its own colours.'

Indeed, the sublimity of his simplicity is such that it is not so much an interpretation as 'an Idea of the World', as Wagner said of music, in his work on Beethoven, 'wherein the world immediately exhibits its essential nature'.

The light he knew was that which illuminates our common earth, but whose source, whose beginning, is beyond our knowledge,—the 'celestial light'.

1. Applicable to Wordsworth

'The Peace of the celestial city is the perfectly ordered and harmonious enjoyment of God and of one another in God. The peace of all things is the tranquillity of order.'—Saint Augustine, *The City of God*.

To this peace, Wordsworth attained.—E. S.

Wordsworth, at his highest, has the tranquillity, the activity of the saints: the 'tranquillity according to His essence, activity according to His Nature: perfect stillness, perfect fecundity' of which Rusbroeck wrote in *De Vera Contemplatione*.

'The nobler things are, the commoner they are. Love is noble, because it is universal.'—Tauler, *Sermons*.

'God is so omnipresent, as that the Ubiquitary will needs have

126

the body of God everywhere; so omnipresent, as that the Stan-carest will needs have God not only to be in everything, but to be everything—that God is an angel in an angel, and a stone in a stone, and a straw in a straw.'—John Donne, Sermon VII.

'Can you take too much joy in your Father's works? He is Himself in everything. Some things are little on the outside, and rough and common, but I remember the time when the dust of the streets were as pleasing as gold to my infant eyes, and now they are more precious to the eye of reason.'—THOMAS TRAHERNE, *Centuries of Meditation.*

'Suppose a river, or a drop of water, an apple, or a sand, an ear of corn, or an herb: God knoweth infinite excellencies in it more than we: He seeth how it relateth to angels and men; how it proceedeth from the most perfect Lover to the most perfect Beloved; how it conduceth in its place, by the best of means to the best of ends: and for this cause it cannot be beloved too much. God the author and God the end are to be beloved in it; angels and men are to be beloved in it; and it is highly to be esteemed for their sakes. O what a treasure is every sand when truly understood! Who can love anything that God made too much. What a world would that be, were everything loved as it ought to be.'—TRAHERNE, *Centuries of Meditation.*

Emerson said of Goethe: 'There is a certain heat in the breast, which attends the perception of a primary truth, which is the shining of the spiritual sun down into the shaft of the mine'.

This was the common experience, also, of Wordsworth.—E. S.

'He ... has a certain gravitation towards truth.'—*Ibid.*

2. On Wordsworth

'The peculiar note of Wordsworth's genius at its very highest, is that of sublimity in tenderness.'—SWINBURNE, *Essays and Studies*.

'The Beatific Vision has come to him in tangible embodied form, through a kind of religion of the eye, which seems to attain its final rapture, unlike most forms of mysticism, with open eyes.'—ARTHUR SYMONS, *The Romantic Movement in English Poetry*.

3. On Certain Flaws in this Great Poet

'... It seems to me undeniable that Wordsworth, who could endow such daily matters, such modest emotion and experience, with a force of contagious and irresistible sympathy which makes their interest universal and eternal, showed no such certitude of hand when dealing with the proper and natural elements of tragedy.'—SWINBURNE, writing on Wordsworth's 'Tribute to the Memory of a Dog'.

'We hate poetry that has a palpable design upon us, and if we do not agree, seems to put its hand into its breeches pocket. ... Old Matthew spoke to him some years ago on some nothing, and because he happens in an evening walk to imagine the figure of the old man, he must stamp it down in black and white, and it is henceforth sacred. I don't mean to deny Wordsworth's grandeur ... but I mean to say we need not be teased with grandeur and merit when we can have them uncontaminated and unobtrusive.'—KEATS, Letter to Reynolds, 3 Feb. 1818.

NOTE.—Lord Houghton, in his Life of Keats, remarks: 'Keats was perhaps unconsciously swayed in his estimate of Wordsworth at this moment by an incident which had happened at Mr. Haydon's. The young poet had been induced to repeat to the elder the Hymn to Pan, out of 'Endymion' … Wordsworth only said, "It was a pretty piece of Paganism." '

NOTE.—A monstrous remark. In any case, Keats' criticism had justice in it, and Wordsworth's had none.—E. S.

'… Part of [his] singular power over certain minds was doubtless owing to the might of will, the solid individual weight of mind, which moulded his work into the form he chose for it; part to the strong assumption and high self-reliance which grew in him so close to the self-confidence and presumption; part to the sublimity and supremacy of his genius in its own climate and proper atmosphere—one which forbids access to all others and escape to him, since only there can he breathe and range, and he alone can breathe and range there; part to the frequent vapour that wraps his head and the frequent dust that soils his feet, filling the softer sort with admiration of one so lofty and so familiar; and part, I fear, to the quality which no great poet shared or can share with him, his inveterate and invincible Philistinism, his full community of spirit, and faith, in certain things of import, with the vulgarest English mind—or that which, with the Philistine, does duty for a mind. To those who, like Shelley and Landor, could mark this indomitable chillness and thickness of sense which makes him mix with magnificent and flawless verse, the "enormous folly "of those stupid staves, his pupils could always point out again the peculiar and unsurpassable grandeur of his higher mood; it was vain to reply that these could be seen and enjoyed without condonation or excuse of his violent and wearisome peculiarities. This is what makes his poetry such unwholesome and immoral reading for Philistines; they can turn upon their rebukers and say, "Here is one of us

129

who by your own admission is also one of the great poets".'—
SWINBURNE, *Essays and Studies*.

'What Wordsworth's poetic life lacked was energy, and he
refused to recognise that no amount of energy will suffice for a
continual production. ... When one has said that he wrote
instinctively, without which there could be no poetry, one must
add that he wrote always. Continual writing is really a bad form
of dissipation; it drains away the very marrow of the brain.'—
ARTHUR SYMONS, *The Romantic Movement in English Poetry*.

4. Of the Differences between Sorrow in the Poems of Wordsworth and Shelley

Of Wordsworth it might be said, 'God places a watery cloud in
the eye, that when the light of heaven shines upon it, it may pro-
duce a rain-bow to be a sacrament'.—JEREMY TAYLOR, in a
Sermon.

To Shelley might be applied the words of St. Ignatius: 'My
Eros is crucified'.

XXVIII

Notes on Shakespeare

These notes on Shakespeare are written with a proper sense of humility and awe. They do not profess to be anything more than a series of notes,—and they deal, often, with technical matters.

In these gigantic works there are the differences in nature, in matter, in light, in darkness, in movement, that we find in the universe. Sometimes the identities of which this world is made belong, as it were, to the separate kingdoms, to the different grades in the series of existence,—to the mineral kingdom, the vegetable kingdom, the brute creation.—Or they are three of the elements: Fire: Lear. Water: Hamlet. Air: Romeo and Juliet. The fourth element is always present! Shakespeare knew that there is no fragment of clay, however little worth, that is not entirely composed of inexplicable qualities.

Characters such as Falstaff are "lumps of the world', are still 'alive from the roots, a part not yet cut off from universal nature', and have 'a gross' physical 'enormity of sensation' which approaches a kind of physical godhead.

Certain characters that we do not see, but that are known to the beings of this world,—Robin Nightwork, for instance, and old Jane Nightwork ('old, old, Master Shallow'), and Cousin Silence, whom we do see,—are like sweet shadows, remembered from youth, and still haunting the brain of that earthy old man, Sir John Falstaff, whose 'redness is from Adam'.

Shakespeare is like the sun, that common-kissing Titan, having 'a passion for matter, pure and impure'—' an energy beyond good and evil, an immense benevolence creating without choice or preference out of the need of giving birth to life. Never was there such a homage to light, to light and the principle of life.'

(NOTE.—This was said by Arthur Symons of a still great, though infinitely lesser artist than Shakespeare, and an artist in a different medium,—Edouard Manet. But it seems still more applicable to Shakespeare.)

He knew all differences in good and evil,—that between the evil of Iago, who, as a devil, is Prince of the Power of the Air ... who, 'as the air works upon our bodies, this Presence works upon our minds',—and the beings of 'Titus Andronicus', the kind of being of whom Donne, in his 41st Sermon, said, 'He is a devil to himself, that could be, and would be, ambitious in a spital, licentious in a wilderness, voluptuous in a famine, and abound with temptations in himself, though there were no devil'.—(This is not one of the greatest of Shakespeare's plays, but has, as Swinburne said of Chapman,' passages of a sublime and Titanic beauty, rebellious and excessive in style as in sentiment, but full of majestic and massive harmony'.)

In the tragedies the theme is, in nearly all cases, the struggle of man against the gigantic forces of nature, or of man brought face to face with the eternal truths. ... The king made equal with the beggar at the feast of the worm. The king whose will has never been combated, under 'the extremities of the skies', the king who

> Striues in his little world of man to outscorne
> The to-and-fro conflicting wind and raine,—

('when the raine came to wet me once and the wind to make me chatter, when the Thunder would not peace at my bidding, there I found'em, there I smelt'em out. Go to, they are not men o' their words: they told me I was euerything:'tis a Lye: I am not Agu-proofe'). ... Macbeth and Lady Macbeth, hunted through the days and nights by the Furies their crime has summoned from the depths ... those Furies who pull down days and nights upon them until light is as darkness, darkness as light:

> MACBETH: ... What is the night?
> LADY MACBETH: Almost at odds with morning, which is which.

Death quenching the light of beauty and of youth, quenching love:

> The iawes of darknesse do deuoure it up
> So quick bright things come to confusion.

Timon of Athens digging with his nails in the wilderness to unearth the most humble roots wherewith to stay his hunger, and finding, not roots, but uneatable gold,—Hamlet and that terrible' globe' his head, that world ruled by so small a star.

King Lear is largely a diatribe against procreation. ... Edgar's

> The Gods are just, and of our pleasant uices
> Make instruments to plague us:

133

The dark and uitious place where thee he got
Cost him his eyes.

Gloucester to Lear:

> … Dost thou know me?

Lear, replying to the eyeless Gloucester:

> I remember thine eyes well enough. Dost thou squinny at
> me? No, doe thy worst, blind Cupid; Ile not loue.

Lear crying

> No, they cannot touch me for coyning:
> I am the King himselfe …

—the coyning to which he refers is, I think, the procreation of his daughters, that base metal.

Yet Man can rise to such a height that he can speak, as an equal, with the gods:

> KENT: Fortune, good night, smile once more, turn thy wheel.

The griefs, the joys, of these vast beings are as those of the elements, of the universe or the heavens.

> Will Caesar weepe?
> > He has a cloud in's face.
> > *(Antony and Cleopatra*, III, 2)

> Her brother's noontide with th' Antipodes.
> > *(Midsummer Nighfs Dream*, III, 2)

Man speaks with the gods, and the answer of the gods sounds through strange mouths … the voice of the Oracle speaks through the lips of two passers-by in the marketplace:

> ' 'Tis uerie like he hath the Falling sicknesse.'
> 'No, Cesar hath it not: but you, and I
> And honest Caska, we haue the Falling sicknesse.'
> 'I know not what you meane by that, but I am sure Cesar
> fell doune. If the rag-tagge people did not clap him, and
> hisse him, according as he pleas'd, and displeas'd them, as
> they use to do the players in the theatre, I am no true man.'

The voice of the Oracle sounds again through the lips of Macbeth's porter. As the knocking at the Castle gate changes to the noise of the damned knocking at the gate of Hell, so that voice changes to that of the porter at Hell's gate,—the Castle is no longer a Castle, but the place of the damned, of that 'Farmer that hang'd himselfe on th' expectation of Plentie'—(the woman to whom the harvest was of the physical world,—who sowed, who reaped and who, in the end, hanged herself when the reaping was done, and she knew the worth of the harvest)—and the man 'who committed Treason enough for God's sake, yet could not equivocate to Heaven: O! come in, Equivocator'. Throughout the tragedies there are strange mutterings, as of a sibyl prophesying doom:

> 'There was such laughing. Queen Hecuba laught till her
> eyes ran ore.'
> '… with Milstones.'
> 'And Cassandra laught.'

Or a ghost turns prophet:

BRUTUS

Why com'st thou?

GHOST

135

To tell thee thou shalt see me at Philippi.

BRUTUS

Well, then I shall see thee againe?

GHOST

I, at Philippi.

BRUTUS

Why, I will see thee at Philippi then.

And from the lips of another ghost sound these words:

And duller should'st thou be than the fat weede
That rots itselfe in ease on Lethe Wharfe.

*   *   *

The beating of these greater hearts, the pulse of this vaster humanity, seem energised by these rhythms, which are like the 'active principles' of which Newton wrote.

Shakespeare's own immense benevolence and love, and the tragedy, the doom which are shadows cast by these huge characters,—(shadows bearing their shape, moving as they act) are conveyed through the world of sound. Through rhythm, which is 'the mind of dance and the skeleton of tone', and through tone, 'which is the heart of man',—'this organic being clothed with the flesh of the world'.

At moments, in the very sound of the verse or the prose, is heard the tread of Doom. The beating of Macbeth's heart changes, suddenly, to the knock of Fate's hand upon the door, in that passage already quoted above, where the porter hears the damned knocking at the gate of Hell.

PORTER: 'Heere's a knocking indeede! If a man were Porter of Hell-gate he should have olde turning the key. Knock, knock, knock. ... But this is too cold for Hell.'

(And why is it too cold for Hell? Because of the coldness of the will that planned the deed? Because the upper circles of Hell are warmed by some human passion, and the Porter knew nothing, as yet, of the nethermost darkness.) Or was it not the tread of Doom, the knocking of the damned souls, that was heard,—but (as Sir Arthur Quiller Couch suggested in *Shakespeare's Workmanship*,[1] 'the sane, clear, broad, ordinary workaday world asserting itself, and none the more relentingly for being workaday, and common and ordinary, and broad, clean and sane'.

If we consider the celestial and terrestrial mechanics of Shakespeare's vast music, at times the movement of the lines is like that slow astronomic rhythm by which the northern and southern atmospheres are alternately subject to greater extremes of temperature. So it is, I think, with *Othello*. Sometimes the verse is frozen into an eternal polar night, as in certain passages of *Macbeth*. Or it has a million varieties of heat and of attraction. Sometimes it is like the sun's heat, as in *Antony and Cleopatra*; sometimes it is the still-retained heat of the earth, as in *Henry IV* and *Henry V*. It moves, like Saturn, in the Dorian mode, like Jupiter in the Phrygian.

Sometimes the gigantic phrases, thrown up by passion, have the character of those geological phenomena, brought about in the lapse of cosmical time, by the sun's heat, by the retained

---

[1] Cambridge University Press.

internal heat of the earth,—or seem part of the earth, fulgurites, rocky substances fused or vitrified by lightning,—as in *Timon of Athens,*—or, as in *Lear,* the words seem thunderbolts, hurled from the heart of heaven. *Lear, Timon of Athens,* seem the works of a god who is compact of earth and fire, or of whom it might be said that he is a fifth element.

The immense differences in shape and character between the caesuras in his verse, and between the pauses that end the lines, have much to do with the variation.

Sometimes the pause is like a whirlpool or vortex, as in the first line of Othello's

> Excellent wretch!   Perdition catch my soul,
> But I do love thee!   And when I love thee not
> Chaos is come again.

Here, between 'wretch!' and 'Perdition', the Caesura has a swirling movement.

But the most wonderful caesura of all occurs in *Macbeth,* as we shall see.

The events in the life of a character, as well as the personality, the very appearance of Shakespeare's men and women, are suggested by the texture, the movement of the lines. In *Macbeth,* for instance, we find, over and over again, schemes of tuneless dropping dissonances. Take the opening of the play:

> FIRST WITCH.
> When shall we three meet againe?
> In thunder, lightning or in raine?
>
> SECOND WITCH
> When the hurly-burly's done,
> When the battle's lost and won.

THIRD WITCH
That will be ere set of Sun.

FIRST WITCH
Where the place?

SECOND WITCH
Upon the heath.

THIRD WITCH
There to meet with Macbeth.

'Done' is a dropping dissonance to 'raine', 'heath' to the second syllable of 'Macbeth',—and these untuned dissonances, falling from the mouths of the three Fates degraded into the shape of filthy hags, have significance. In this vast world torn from the universe of eternal night, there are three tragic themes. The first theme is that of the actual guilt, and the separation in damnation of the two characters,—of the man who, in spite of his guilt, walks the road of the spirit, and who loves the light he has forsaken,—of the woman who, after that invocation to the 'Spirits who tend on mortall thoughts', walks in the material world, and who does not know that light exists, until she is nearing the end and must seek the comfort of one small taper to illumine all the murkiness of Hell. That small taper is the light of her soul. The second tragic theme is of the man's love for this woman whose damnation is of the earth and who is unable, therefore, to conceive of the damnation of the spirit,—and who, in her blindness, strays away from him, leaving him for ever to his lonely hell. The third tragic theme is the woman's despairing love for the man whose vision she cannot see, and whom she has helped to drive into damnation.

The very voices of these two damned souls have therefore a

different sound. His voice is that of some gigantic being in torment,—of a lion with a human soul. In her speech invoking darkness, the actual sound is so murky and thick that the lines seem impervious to light, and, at times rusty, as though they had lain in the blood that had been spilt, or in some hell-borne dew.

There is no escape from what we have done. The past will return to confront us. And even that is shown in the verse. In that invocation there are perpetual echoes, sometimes far removed from each other, sometimes placed close together.

For instance, in the line

> And fill me from the Crowne to the Toe, top-full,

'full' is a darkened dissonance to 'fill'—and these dissonances, put at opposite ends of the line—together with the particular placing of the alliterative *f*'s of 'fill' and 'full', and the alliterative *t*'s—and the rocking up and down of the dissonantal *o*'s ('Crowne', 'Toe', 'top')—show us a mind reeling on the brink of madness, about to topple down into those depths, yet striving to retain its balance.

Let us examine the passage for a moment. I have numbered the stressed assonances because the manner in which they are placed is largely responsible for the movement, and because the texture is extremely variable,—murky always, excepting for a few flares from the fires of Hell, but varying in the thickness of that murk.

> . . . The Rauen himselfe is hoarse
> That croakes the fatall entrance of Duncan
> Under my Battlements.   Come you Spirits,

140

That tend on mortall thoughts, unsex me here, (dissonance to ' dire ')

And fill me from the Crowne to the Toe, top-full (unmated sound) (diss. to ' fill ')

Of direst Crueltie ; make thick my blood, (diss. to ' spirits ')

Stop up th' access and passage to Remorse,

That no compunctious uisitings of Nature

Shake my fell purpose, nor keepe peace betweene

The effect and it.   Come to my Womans Brests,

And take my Milke for Gall, you murth'ring Ministers, (diss. to ' dire ')

Where-euer in your sightlesse substances

You wait on Nature's Mischiefe.   Come thick Night,

And pall thee in the dunnest smoake of Hell,

That my keene knife see not the Wound it makes, (unmated)

Nor Heauen peepe through the blanket of the darke, (diss. to ' thicke ')

To cry, ' Hold, Hold.'

Throughout the whole of the speech, an untuned and terrible effect is produced by these discordant dissonantal *o*'s used outwardly and inwardly in the lines,—'hoarse' rising to 'croakes', thickening to 'come', darkening to 'mortall thoughts' and then— supreme example, making the line rock up and down, and finally topple over, in

And fill me from the Crowne to the Toe, top-full.

'Blood', 'Stop', 'Remorse', 'Come', each of these dissonantal *o*'s has a different height or depth, a different length or choked shortness.

There is a fabric, too, of dull and rusty vowels, thickened *m*'s and *p*'s, and of unshaping *s*'s,—these latter are un-shaping because they are placed close together, and so deprive the line of form, to some degree, as in

141

> Stop up th' access and passage to Remorse
> That no compunctious uisitings of Nature

or

> Where-euer, in your sightlesse substances

Throughout the passage, the consonants are for ever thickening and then thinning again,—perhaps as the will hardens and then, momentarily, dissolves. In the lines

> That croakes the fatall entrance of Duncan
> Under my Battlements. Come you Spirits.

'Come' is a thickened assonance to the *Dun* of 'Duncan' and of the first syllable of 'under'. And in the line

> That no compunctious uisitings of Nature

the first syllable of 'compunctious' is a sort of darkened, thickened reverberation of the word 'come' (darkened or thickened because what follows throws a shade backward); the second syllable is a thickened echo of the first syllable of 'Duncan'.

As the giant shuttles of Fate weave, closening and opening, so do the lines of this speech seem to close and open, and to change their length. But this change is in appearance only, and not real. By this I mean, there are no extra syllables to the line. The apparent change is due to the brightening and lengthening of the vowel sounds. For though, as I have said already, the words are frequently dull and rusty in this passage, at times they rise to a harsh shriek, which sometimes is sustained, sometimes broken,— as with those broken echoes 'Raven', 'fatall'.

There are moments, too, when the line is prolonged for other reasons than that of the changing vowel lengths:

> And take my Milke for Gall, you murth'ring Ministers

is an example. Here, in spite of the fact that all the vowels are dulled (with the exception of the high *a* of 'take' and the dark *a* of 'Gall'), the l's prolong the line slightly, the thick muffled reverberations of the alliterative *m*'s, placed so close together, produce a peculiar effect of dulled horror.

> Stop up th' access and passage to Remorse,

we shall find that instead of the line being slowed (and therefore, in appearance, lengthened) by the *s*'s the dull assonantal *a*'s, a more powerful factor, when placed close together, actually shorten the line, which, again, is thickened by the *p*'s ending words that are placed side by side. The effect produced on a line by *p*'s ending a word, and *p*'s beginning a word, is completely different. A *p* beginning a word does not necessarily thicken the line.

Sometimes the particular placing of the assonances produces a sound like that of a fevered, uneven pulse,—an example is the effect brought about by the drumming of the dull *Un* ... *om* sounds in the lines

Duncan

Under my Battlements.   Come ...

This terrible drumming sound is heard over and over again throughout the passage, and is due not only to the placing of the assonances, but also to the particular placing of double-syllabled and—(this has a still stronger effect)—treble-syllabled words and quick-moving unaccented one-syllabled words. In the line

> And fill me from the Crowne to the Toe, top-full,

'to the' is an example of the effect of these quick-moving unaccented one-syllabled words.

143

is an example of the use of three-syllabled words, disturbing (purposely) the movement of the line.

This march towards Hell is slow, and has a thunderous darkened pomp. It is slow, and yet it has but few pauses,—(for that march is of her own will, she is driven by that will, as by a Fury),—and those pauses are not long, but deep, like fissures opening down into Hell. There is, however, a stretching pause, after the word 'Gall'.

The speeches of Macbeth have a different sound from this. He, at least, would retreat from the path. His dark and terrible voice is not covered by a blood-dewed rust, is not like a black and impenetrable smoke from Hell, as is the voice of the woman who, to him, is Fate,—it is hollow like the depths into which he has fallen, it returns ever, though it, too, has discordances, to one note, dark as the Hell through which he walks with that sleepless soul. The sound is ever: 'No more. Cawdor shall sleep no more, Macbeth shall sleep no more'.

Dr. A. C. Bradley, in his *Shakespearean Tragedy*[2] calls our attention to the three beings in one who must suffer that damnation. 'What he' (Macbeth) 'heard was the voice that first cried "Macbeth does murther sleepe",—and then, a minute later, with a change of tense, denounced on him, as if his three names gave him three personalities to suffer in the doom of sleeplessness:

Glamis hath murihered Sleepe, and therefore Cawdor
Shall sleepe no more, Macbeth shall sleepe no more.'

The despair of Macbeth, hearing the voice that cries those

---

[2] Macmillan.

words, his sense that there is no escape, is brought home to us by the dark, hollow, ever-recurrent echoes of the *or* ... *aw* sounds. That is the keynote of the whole speech. As with Lady Macbeth's speech, the magnificence of the rhythm is largely controlled by the particular places in which the alliterations and assonances are placed—(though in the two speeches they are used completely differently, and have an utterly different effect).

MACBETH

Me thought I heard a voyce cry 'Sleepe no more.
Macbeth does murther Sleepe.' the innocent Sleepe,
Sleepe, that knits up the rauel'd Sleave of Care,
The death of each Daye's life, sore Labor's Bath,
Balme of hurt mindes, great Nature's second Course,
Chief Nourisher in Life's Feast,—

LADY MACBETH

What doe you meane?

MACBETH

Still it cry'd 'Sleepe no more!' to all the House:
'Glamis hath murther'd Sleepe, and therefore Cawdor
Shall sleepe no more, Macbeth shall sleepe no more!'

Twice, a word shudders in that dark voice. The first time it is the word 'innocent'—that word which must henceforth fly from the voice that uttered it.

Sometimes an awe-inspiring, drum-beating sound is heard;— once it is slow, and is caused by placing alliterative *b*'s, with near-assonantal vowel sounds,—'Bath', 'Balme'—at the end of one line and the beginning of the next. (There is a strong pause between these words.) The reason why these *a*'s are not an exact assonance is because of the differences in thickness between the *th* and the *lm*. Then, for a second time, two *a* sounds are placed close together, 'great Nature's', and here the beat is less emphatic; there is no pause between the sounds.

But above all, the quickened beat of a terror-stricken heart is heard in 'therefore Cawdor' ('fore' being a darkened dissonance to 'there', and the two other syllables being as nearly as possible assonances to 'fore',—though 'Caw' is in a slight degree less dark). This is followed by the long, stately, and inexorable march of Doom:

> Shall sleepe no more, Macbeth shall sleepe no more.

It is in this scene that we first become aware of the different paths of damnation,—the path of the spirit that sees that not all great Neptune's Ocean will wash the blood clean from his hand,—and that of the earth-bound Fate who, until she is near her end, dreams that 'a little water cleares us of this deed', and who, when the voice cries

> Cawdor
> Shall sleepe no more, Macbeth shall sleepe no more,

hears only the small voice of the cricket,—or a dark, but still human voice.

> MACBETH
> I have done the deed.   Didst thou not hear a noyse?
>
> LADY MACBETH
> I heard the Owle schreame, and the Crickets cry.
> Did not you speake?

MACBETH

When?

LADY MACBETH

Now.

MACBETH

As I descended?

LADY MACBETH

Aye.

MACBETH

Hearke.
Who lyes i' the second chamber?

LADY MACBETH

Donalbaine.

From now onward, only blood, and the road that he must
tread, exist for Macbeth in the physical world:

Who lyes i' the second chamber?

—who must be the next to fall under his blood-stained hands,
upon that road? ... But to Lady Macbeth, he is speaking, not of
a grave that must be dug, and of a man about to die, but of one
sleeping in his bed,—Donalbaine.

Here then, in those few lines, these two guilt-stricken souls say
farewell for ever. The immense pause after Lady Macbeth's 'Aye'
is a gap in time, like the immense gap between the Ice Age and
the Stone Age, wherein, as science tells us, 'the previously exist-
ing inhabitants of the earth are almost wholly destroyed, and a
different class of inhabitants created'.—On the other side of
that gap in time, Macbeth rises as the new inhabitant of a

147

changed world,—and alone in the universe of eternal night, although the voice of Lady Macbeth, his Fate, that loving Fury, still drives him onward.

Here we have one gigantic use of the pause. Before the words that follow Lady Macbeth's' Donalbaine'—

MACBETH (*looking at his hands*)
This is a sorry sight,

the four beats falling upon the silence until Macbeth speaks, seem like the sound of blood dripping, slowly, from those hands:

What Hands are here! Hah! they plucke out mine Eyes.

Those hands are the hands of murder. They are no longer the hands of the living man who was once Macbeth,—hands made to caress with, hands made to open windows on to the sun and air, hands made to lift the life-giving food to the mouth. Those hands have now given him darkness for ever,—a darkness surrounded by a terrible and all-seeing light, that knows every action, and that yet has no part in him.

Let us take the scene where the ghost of Banquo returns for the second time, to confront his murderer:

MACBETH

Auaunt! and quit my sight! Let the earth hide thee!
Thy bones are marrowless, thy blood is cold;
Thou hast no speculation in those eyes
Which thou dost glare with.

LADY MACBETH

Think of this, good peers,
But as a thing of custom:'tis no other;

148

Only it spoils the pleasure of the time.

MACBETH

     What man dare, I dare:
Approach thou like the rugged Russian bear,
The arm'd rhinoceros or the Hyrcan tyger;
Take any shape but that, and my firm nerves
Shall never tremble: or be alive again,
And dare me to the desert with thy sword;
If trembling I inhabit then, protest me
The baby of a girl. Hence, horrible shadow!
Unreal mockery, hence!—Why, so, being gone,
I am a man againe. Pray you, sit still.

In these lines we hear again that terror-maddened drum-beating of a heart—produced, as before, by the varying use of alliteration, of assonances and near-assonances placed close together within the lines: 'firm nerves', 'never tremble', 'rugged Russian', 'Take any shape'. The feeling of unendurably tautened, sharpened nerves is produced by the particular use of vowels that are tuned just above the pitch of almost identical vowels in the preceding word: 'Hyrcan tyger', for instance. The change from 'firm nerves' to the higher discordances of 'Hyrcan tyger', is another example. 'Sight' is a rising dissonance to 'quit'—rising as terror rises. 'Hide' is an assonance to 'sight', but is longer, because of the *d*.

Further on in the passage there are the dissonances 'girl', 'unreal'—(the latter being, as it were, a broken crumbling shadow of the sound of 'girl')—and the rising dissonances 'gone', 'againe'. All these general discordances add to the impression of a nature alternately sharpened and untuned by fear.

Internally and externally in the lines there are far-separated,

149

but still insistent, echoes, and these help, in part, to keep the slow sound together: 'glare', 'dare', 'bear'—with Lady Macbeth's less-long, discordant, lower 'peers'.

In the last line:

> I am a man againe. Pray you, sit still,

there is practically no shape, excepting that given by the caesura, which is a chasm dividing the line. The doom-haunted man has lost even the sound of his own heart-beat.

After this scene, the gulf separating these two giant beings is impassable. Not only the change of the world in which they live, but the whole depth of the soul, separate them. They are divided in all but love. From that time, I think even the appearance of Macbeth must have inspired terror, as if he were no longer a mortal man, but one of those giant comets whom Pliny named Crinatae, 'shaggy with bloody locks ... having the appearance of a fleece surmounted with a kind of crown,—or one that prognosticates high winds and great heat ... they are also visible in the winter months and about the South Pole, but they have no rays proceeding from them'.

And Lady Macbeth,—how changed is she, in that pitiful scene when she, who had cried to 'thicke Night' to envelop the world and her, she who had rejected light, seeks the comfort of one little taper,—the small candle-flame of her soul, to light all the murkiness of Hell. Yet still, in the lonely mutterings of one who must walk through Hell alone, save for the phantom of Macbeth, we hear that indomitable will that pushed him to his doom, rising once more in the vain hope that she may shield and guide him.

There is, in these two beings, the giant faithfulness of the Lion and his mate.

To speak of this scene from a technical point of view, the

extremely interesting theory was propounded by Mr. A. M. Bayfield (*A Study of Shakespeare's Versification*: Cambridge University Press) that 'Lady Macbeth's speeches, which have always been printed as prose, are really verse, and very fine verse too. The reader' (he continues) 'will see how enormously they gain by being delivered in measure, and that the lines drawn out in monosyllabic feet are as wonderfully effective as any that Shakespeare wrote.

'But for the retention of the iambic scheme, the recognition would doubtless have been made long ago, but editors recognise no monosyllabic foot and would hesitate to produce lines with initial trochees.'

The speeches in the sleep-walking scene, if spoken as verse, have a great majesty: they drag the slow weight of the guilt along as if it were the train of pomp. But they have not the infinite pathos of the speeches when they are in prose, they do not inspire the same pity for this vast being, her gigantic will relaxed by sleep, trying to draw that will together as she wanders through the scenes of her crime. The more relaxed sound of the prose produces that effect. The beat of the verse should be felt, rather than heard, underlying the speeches.

Macbeth, too, has changed. That change came when he, alone, heard the voice, and knew that he was alone for ever. He who, in the midst of the darkness in that giant universe his soul, could yet love the light, is about to turn from it, for he is about to undergo the Mesozoic Age, the Age of Stone:

> I gin to be aweary of the Sun.

And after the piteous human longing of

> Cure her of that.
> Canst thou not minister to a mind diseas'd,
> Plucke from the memory a rooted sorrow,

151

> Raze out the written troubles of the braine,
> And with some sweet obliuious antidote
> Cleanse the stuff'd bosom of that perilous stuff
> Which weighs upon the heart?

the words

> She should have died hereafter;
> There would have been a time for such a word

—in their very quietness, their slowness, those tears shed in the soul by those lidless eyes seem an ablation, the wasting of a rock or glacier by water-dropping, by melting.

Those two beings have passed even from the darkness of a world in which it was possible to ask

> Is't night's predominance, or the day's shame,
> That darkness does the face of Earth entomb,
> When living light should kiss it?

—a darkness of which they have become so much natives that day and night are as one:

MACBETH

> What is the night?

LADY MACBETH

> Almost at odds with morning, which is which,

and that yet is illumined by the vision of a lost heaven,—a heaven that lives yet in spite of their fall:

> Angels are bright although the brightest fell.

From the vast universe that was Shakespeare's mind, he produces all degrees of light and of darkness. Here then, at the end of the tragedy, we have a region like that of the Poles, where there is perpetual darkness.

In *King Lear* we have, first, the furious blackness of a typhoon, carrying worlds before it, then a long and prodigious Eclipse of the Sun, then peace. But over the world of *Hamlet*, unlike the worlds of *Macbeth* and of *Lear*, reigns a perpetual and terible light,—the light of truth, dissolving all into its elements. 'In Syene,' wrote Pliny, 'south of Alexandria ... a little north of the tropics ... there is no shadow at noon, on the day of the solstice. ... In those places in India where there are no shadows ... the people there do not reckon time by hours ... So, in *Hamlet*, that world of the terrible light in which even the dead cannot rest in the peace of the grave, there is no time: the beat of verse sometimes loses its pulse, dissolves in the light changes to the shadowless, Timeless clime of prose.

Nothing may rest in darkness.

Writing of the question of 'the old mole', Professor Dover Wilson (in *What Happened in Hamlet*: Cambridge University Press) wrote that Reginald Scott's *Discourses of Witchcraft*, to which he appended 'A Discourse upon Diuels and Spirits', is 'recognised by all as one of Shakespeare's source books. Scott tells us that "the worst moiety of diuels" were divided into Acquei, Subterranei and Lucifegi, and declares that the Subterranei "assault them that are miners or pioneers, which use to worke in deepe and darke holes under the earth" ("Discourse", chap. 3).' Professor Dover Wilson adds: 'we may remember too that Sir Toby Belch speaks of the Devil as "a foul collier". After all this, is it not clear that Hamlet's words,

> Well said, old mole! canst work i' th' earth so fast?
> A worthy pioner!

identify the mutterings of the Ghost with the rumblings of one "of those demons that are … underground", to quote Milton?'

Probably. But may not the meaning be even deeper than that? Is not the 'earth' of which Hamlet speaks, his own 'too sullied' flesh, his body, in which many things that were hidden are now thrown up by that old mole, into the light?

Consider the raging darkness, the furious whirlwind sweep of the second scene on the Heath in *King Lear*,—those gigantic lines in which Lear defies the whole heaven, cries to it to blot out the world:

> Blow, windes, and cracke your cheeks! rage! blow!
> You Cataracts, and Hyrricanos, spout,
> Till you have drench'd our Steeples, drown'd the Cockes!
> You Sulphurous and Thought-executing Fires,
> Uaunt-curriers to Oake-cleauing Thunder-bolts,
> Sindge my white head! And thou, all-shaking Thunder,
> Strike flat the thicke Rotundity o' the world,
> Cracke Natures moulds, all germaines spill at once
> That make ingratefull Man.

The verse has variety as vast as the theme. The first line is an eight-syllabled one; then, under the sweep of this enormous rage, stretching from pole to pole, the lines rush forward into decasyllabics and even hendecasyllabics—(and this is not always, though it is sometimes, the result of pretended elision).

The movement is hurled backward and forward. In the first line, for instance, of those strong monosyllables 'rage', 'blow', the first sweeps onward across the world into infinity, the second is hurled backward. In

You Sulphurous and Thought-executing Fires

the vowel-sounds mount, like a rising fury, then the word 'Fires' (with its almost, but not quite, double-syllabled sound) gives again, though with a different movement, the effect of stretching across the firmament.

Part of the immensity of this vast primeval passage is due to the fact that in the line

Uaunt-curriers to Oake-cleauing Thunder-bolts

the only word that does not bear an accent is 'to',—and part, again, is due to the contrast between the stretching one-syllabled words of the first line and the three-syllabled 'Cataracts' and four-syllabled 'Hyrricanos' of the second. Added vastness is given by the balance between the high *a* of 'rage' and that of 'Hyrricanos', and by the huge fall from the *a*, in this latter word, to that word's last syllable. Variety in this ever-changing, world-wide tempest is given, too, by the long menacing roll, (in the midst of those reverberating thunder-claps the *c*'s and *ck*'s of the whole passage)—the roll, gradually increasing in sound, of the first three words in

And thou, all-shaking Thunder,

rising and stretching to the long first syllable of 'shaking' and then falling from that enormous height to the immense, long, thickened darkness of the word 'Thunder'.

Compare this raging blackness with the Stygian, smirching darkness of Lear's invective on Woman,—a darkness that first has shape, but then crumbles, falls, at last, into that chaos in which the world will end. It is not for nothing that the vastly formed verse gutters down into an unshaped prose.

155

I, euery inch a King:

When I doe stare, see how the Subject quakes.

I pardon that mans life. What was thy cause?

Adultery?

Thou shalt not dye: dye for Adultery! No:

The Wren goes too't, and the small gilded Fly

Do's letcher in my sight.

Let Copulation thriue; for Gloucester's bastard Son

Was kinder to his Father than my Daughters

Got'tweene the lawfull sheets.

Too't Luxury, pell-mell! for I lacke Souldiers.

Behold yond simp'ring Dame,

Whose face between her forkes presages snow;

That minces Uertue, and does shake the head

To heare of pleasure's name;

The Fitchew nor the soyled Horse goes too't

With a more riotous appetite.

Downe from the waste they are Centaures,

Though Women all aboue:

But to the Girdle doe the Gods inherit,

Beneath is all the Fiends'.

There's hell, there's darknesse, there is the sulphurous pit;

Burning, scalding, stench, consumption; Fye, fye, fie!
pah, pah! Giue me an ounce of Ciuet, good Apothe-
cary, to sweeten my imagination: there's money for
thee.

GLOUCESTER

O! let me kisse that hand.

156

LEAR

Let me wipe it first;
It smelles of Mortality.

That world of eternal night, *King Lear*, contains all degrees of
darkness: the advance into night of
Childe Rowland to the darke tower came,

—a night of mystery. Both the quartos print this alternative:

Childe Rowland to the darke *towne* came.

It is not for me to pronounce on the rightness or wrongness of
this, when men who are learned have judged it better not to do
so. But my instinct (and this alone can guide me) tells me that
'towne' may have been in that giant mind, and that certain rea-
sons may have led to the change to 'tower'.

If he wrote 'towne', then we know, beyond any doubt, what he
meant. The dark towne is Death. But the reasons for the change
may have been these. In the dark *towne* the roofs are low; our
house is our coffin. We are huddled together, are one of a nation,
are equal.

If we come to the dark *tower*, we are alone with our soul. The
roof is immeasurably high,—as high as heaven. In that eternal
solitude there are echoes.

Consider the change from the anguish of

You do me wrong to take me out o' the graue:
Thou art a soule in blisse, but I am bound
Upon a wheele of fire, that mine own teares
Do scald, like molten Lead,

to the gentleness, the consoling and tender darkness of these

157

lines, spoken by one to whom a world-wide ruin has, in the end, taught wisdom and resignation:

> No, no, no, no! Come let's away to prison;
> We two alone will sing like Birds i' the Cage:
> When thou dost aske me blessing, Ile kneele downe
> And aske of thee forgiueness: So wee'l liue,
> And pray, and sing, and tell old tales, and laugh
> At gilded Butterflies: and heere poor Rogues
> Talke of Court newes, and wee'l talke with them too,
> Who looses, and who wins; who's in, who's out;
> And take upon us the mystery of things,
> As if we were God's spies: and wee'l weare out
> In a wall'd prison, packs and sects of great ones,
> That ebbe and flowe by the moone.

Here, part of the gentleness, the moving sweetness, is given by the fact that in the double-syllabled and three-syllabled words, in every case excepting in two, ('gilded Butterflies',) every hard consonant there may be is softened by an *s*, 'prison', 'blessing', 'forgiueness', 'mystery'.

The passages which come immediately before the death of Cordelia have all this heart-breaking sweetness. Is there another poet in the world who would have dared the use of that five-times-repeated trochee in the second line quoted below:

> ... Thou'lt come no more,
> Neuer, neuer, neuer, neuer, neuer

—trochees that with each repetition seem dropping further into darkness? Is there another poet in the world who could have wrung from the simple repetition of one word such tears?

It is this absolute simplicity, this apparent plainness of

statement beneath which lies the depth of the whole world, which makes part of his greatness: Lear touching the cheek of Cordelia, wondering: 'Be your teares wet?' and knowing, by those tears, that she lives yet, and is not a phantom returned to him from beyond the grave; Iago's

> ... Not Poppy, nor Mandragora,
> Nor all the drowsie Syrrups of the world,
> Shall euer medicine thee to that sweete sleepe
> Which thou owd'st yesterday;

Othello's

> ... Oh now, for ever
> Farewell the Tranquill minde; farewell Content,
> Farewell the plumed Troope and the big warres.

This is the primal simplicity that yet holds within it the possibilities of all variations of form. His pulse is the vast rhythm that holds the worlds together, that holds the stars in their orbits.

In *Antony and Cleopatra* the darkness is not that of a night haunted by the Furies, and lit by the flares of Hell, but is like the beauty of one who said

> ... think on me
> That am with Phoebus' amorous pinches black,
> And wrinckled deep in time.

This night of death, into which the splendours of the day, hung with a million suns, must sink, the night in which the warrior unarms, his task done, to find sleep by the side of his lover, is a smiling darkness.

> Finish, good lady, the bright day is done,
> And we are for the dark.

This softness, this languor, this dark magnificence shapes the movement, lies on the last scenes like the bloom on the fruit. Even the scene with the Clown who brings death in a basket of figs, has this strange and smiling bloom, the peacefulness of death that is no more fearful than the shining darkness that lies on the figs:

CLEOPATRA

> Hast thou the pretty worm of Nilus there
> That kills and pains not?

CLOWN

> Truly I haue him; but I would not be the party that should
>   desire you to touch him, for his biting is immortal. …
>   I wish you all joy of the worm.

In the slow-moving pomp and splendour of the verse in the scene of Cleopatra's death, all the vowel-sounds, at the beginning of the passage, are dark and full, and these vowels are, in part, the cause of the movement, because they bring about the pauses:

CLEOPATRA

> Giue me my Robe, put on my Crowne; I haue
> Immortall longings in me: Now no more
> The juyce of Egypts Grape shall moyst this lip.
> Yare, yare, good Iras; quicke. Me thinkes I heare
> Antony call: I see him rowse himselfe
> To praise my Noble Act; I heare him mocke

The lucke of Cesar, which the gods giue men
To excuse their after wrath. Husband, I come;
Now to that name, my courage proue my Title!
I am Fire, and Ayre; my other Elements
I giue to baser life. So; have you done?
Come then, and take the last warmth of my lippes.
Farewell, kinde Charmian; Iras, long farewell.

(Kisses them. Iras falls and dies).
Haue I the Aspicke in my lips? Dost fall?
If thou and Nature can so gently part,
The stroke of death is as a Louer's pinch,
Which hurts, and is desir'd. Dost thou lie still?
If thus thou uanishest, thou tell'st the world,
It is not worth leaue-taking.

CHARMIAN

Dissolue, thick Cloud, and Raine; that I may say,
The gods themselves doe weepe.

CLEOPATRA

This proues me base:
If she first meet the curled Antony,
Hee'l make demand of her, and spend that kisse
Which is my heauen to haue. Come, thou mortall wretch,
(To the asp, which she places at her breast.)
With thy sharpe teeth this knot intrinsicate,
Of life at once untie: Poore uenemous Foole,
Be angry, and despatch. Oh couldst thou speeke,
That I might heere thee call great Caesar Asse
Unpolicied.

CHARMIAN

Oh Easterne starre!

CLEOPATRA

           Peace, peace!
Dost thou not see my Baby at my breast,
That suckes the Nurse asleepe?

CHARMIAN

O breake! O breake!

CLEOPATRA

As sweet as Balme, as soft as Ayre, as gentle,—
O Antony! Nay I will take thee too,
           (Applying another asp to her arm.)
What should I stay—   *(Dies.)*

CHARMIAN

           In this uile world? So fare thee well!
Now boast thee Death, in thy possession lies
A Lasse unparallel'd. Downy Windowes, cloze;
And golden Phoebus neuer be beheld
Of eyes again so Royall! Your Crownes awry;
Ile mend it, and then play. …

In the lines with which Cleopatra's speech begins:

Giue me my Robe, put on my Crowne; I haue
Immortall longings in me; Now no more,

162

—the first line has the same two long dissonantal *o*'s as in the first line of Lady Macbeth's

> And fill me from the Crowne to the Toe, top-full
> Of direst Cruelties; make thicke my blood

—but the place of the dissonances is reversed, and the effect is utterly different. This is due, in part, to the hard *t*'s of Lady Macbeth's lines, and to the *k* and *ck* of 'make thicke'. Also, in the second line of Lady Macbeth's, the vowels are not deep, dark, and rich as are those in the second line of Cleopatra's. In

> Giue me my Robe, put on my Crowne; I haue

the long magnificence of the *o*'s, the first being rich and deep, but not dark, the second effulgent with brightening jewels,— these darken to the splendour of the *o*'s in the second line,—that in 'immortall' being the deepest; that in 'longing', in spite of the *g* which gives it poignancy, is soft because of the *n*. The *o* of 'now' echoes (though the length is less) the *o* of 'Crowne', 'more' echoes the *or* of 'immortall', and indeed throughout the first lines there are echoes, some lengthening, some dying away, some more air-thin than the sound of which they are a memory, because of the difference between the consonants that embody the vowels. And these echoes give the verse the miraculous soft balance of the whole.

For instance, 'lucke' in the 7th line is a dulled dissonance to 'quicke' in the 4th, and is divided from this by the darker, more hollow dissonance of 'mocke' in the 5th. 'Praise', in the 6th line, is a higher dissonantal echo of 'rowse' in the 5th, and 'Come', the first word of the 11th line, is an echo of 'done', the last word in the 10th. But an echo that has taken on a body. Again, in the lines

... this proues me base:
If she first meet the curled Antony,
Hee'l make demand of her, and spend that kisse
Which is my heauen to haue,

the miraculous balance is due to the dissonances 'base' and
'kisse', and the alliterative *b*'s of 'heauen' and 'haue'. In that
wonder of poetry:

CHARMIAN

Oh Easterne starre!

CLEOPATRA

Peace, peace!
Dost thou not see my Baby at my breast,
That suckes the Nurse asleepe?

CHARMIAN

O breake! O breake!

CLEOPATRA

As sweet as Balme, as soft as Ayre, as gentle,

—(the Easterne starre is Venus, the star of the east, and is also
Cleopatra: is, too, the rising star of death, all three in one—) the
beauty of the sound is due to the balance of the poignant *e*'s,—
these changing to dimmed *e*'s, to the particular arrangement in
which they are placed, and, also, to the placing and balancing of
the two-syllabled words: the long *e*'s of 'asleepe' are a reversed echo
of the long *e* of 'Easterne'; the *e* of 'gentle' is dimmed and softened.
The arrangement of the *s*'s gives a feeling of strange gentleness,

164

and the fact that they are often alliterative gives balance.

The texture of the passage is for ever darkening and softening, then brightening and becoming poignant once more: 'breast', for instance, is a higher echo of the dusky, softened 'dost'—'ayre' is a softened, bodiless, wavering, dissonantal echo of the shorter, sharper 'starre'.

In the first three lines of that passage which begins with the words 'In this uile world' there is a lovely pattern of *l*'s, gentle and languorous; the beauty of the dropping dissonances 'uile' 'well'; 'lies', 'Lasse', 'cloze', is very great. And it is these, the occasional alliterations ('world' 'well' lies 'Lasse'), the echoing *o*'s placed close together, of 'Windowes', 'cloze', 'golden', and the perpetual ground-sound (if I may so express it) of *i*'s and *y*'s,— 'uile', 'lies', 'eyes', 'awry', together with the particular arrangement of assonantal dim *e*'s,—'well'. 'Death', 'possession', 'beheld' mend'. which give the passage its flawless balance.

An extraordinary beauty and strangeness is given, in the last four lines of that passage, by the difference in balance and length of the double-syllabled words—the first syllable of 'Downy' and 'Windowes' being not quite equal, for the *ow* of 'downy' is longer,—the first syllables of 'golden' and 'Phoebus' being equal, and 'Royall' being less a word of two syllables than a word of one and three quarters.

In the midst of the youthful warmth, the eternal moonlight of the *Midsommer Nights Dreame*, we find these lines whose richness and dark splendour, graver than the rest of the play, might have grown, as far as its movement, its slow magnificence, are concerned, in *Antony and Cleopatra;* although the lovers of the Midsummer Night are younger than Antony and his Queen: it is a youthful passion that speaks, not luxury:

165

LYSANDER

The course of true loue neuer did runne smoothe;
But either it was different in bloud,—

HERMIA

O crosse! too high to be in thralled to loue!

LYSANDER

Or else misgraffed, in respect of yeares,

HERMIA

O spight! Too olde to be ingag'd to young.

LYSANDER

Or else, it stood upon the Choyce of friends,

HERMIA

O hell! to choose loue by another's eyes.

LYSANDER

Or if there were a sympathy in choyce,
Warre, death or sicknesse did lay siege to it,
Making it momentany as a sound,
Swift as a shadowe, short as any dreame,
Briefe as the lightning in the collied night,
That, in a spleene, unfolds both heauen and earth,
And, ere a man hath power to say 'beholde',
The iawes of darknesse do deuoure it up;
So quicke bright things come to confusion.

The miraculous shape of this is largely due to the particular placing of the alliterative *s*'s—each word containing an *s* sound having its own particular shape, height, or depth, its own degree of sharpness—(this last effect being given by an attached *h*), its own peculiar length or shortness, softness or body. These variations have much effect upon the rhythm. The first syllables of 'sympathy' and 'sicknesse', for instance, although the *y* and the *i* are assonances, are not equal in length. 'Sympathy' has a fairly long, stretching, first syllable, and it remains on a level, whereas the first syllable of 'sicknesse' is, though very slightly, shorter: it is also rounded by the *ck*. There is a drop from 'siege' to 'sound'. 'Sound' is longer than 'swift' and has a different shape,—it stretches into space and then dies away again, whilst 'swift', though short, has the faintest possible movement *within* its one syllable, owing to the *f*, which is, however, stopped, as soon as heard, by the *t*. 'Spleene', again, is so long a word, owing to the stretching *e*'s, that although, actually, it has but one syllable, it almost equals, in length, a word of two syllables.

The shape is largely the result, too, of the alliterative *d*'s of 'darknesse' and 'deuoure'—alliterations that gather the rhythm together. But above all, the movement of this wonderful passage is given by the changing vowel-lengths, brightening and lengthening, dimming and shrinking, and by the particular place in which the assonances and dissonances are put,—(the change from the youthful warmth of the sound of those assonances 'bloud' and 'loue', the heightening despair of 'choose' 'eyes').

Then there is the darkening of the sound from 'spleene' to 'man' (these dissonances being placed in exactly the same position in the line), the brilliant sharpness of 'quicke bright'; then the dulling-down to the thickness of 'come' and the dusty shapelessness of 'confusion'—the drop into darkness, into chaos, of those last words 'come to confusion'.

167

Let us turn from this dark magnificence to the sweet flickering shadows—(the years are but these)—cast by the summer sun over the quick-running, water-chuckling, repetitive talk of the old woman to whom,

Sitting in the sun under the doue-house wall,

the Earthquake was no more than the shaking of the dove-house as the doves prepare to fly.

NURSE

Euen or odd, of all daies in the yeare,
Come Lammas Eve at night shall she be fourteene.
Susan and she—God rest all Christian soules,
Were of an age. Well, Susan is with God;
She was too good for me. But as I said,
On Lammas Eve at night shall she be fourteene;
That shall she, marrie; I remember it well.
Tis since the Earth-quake now eleven yeares;
And she was wean'd, I neuer shall forget it,
Of all the daies in the yeare upon that day;
For I had then laide worme-wood to my dug,
Sitting in the sun under the Doue-house wall.
My Lord and you were then at Mantua.
Nay, I doo beare a braine:—But, as I said,
When it did taste the worme-wood on the nipple
Of my dug, and felt it bitter, prettie foole,
To see it teachie and fall out with the Dugge.
'Shake,' quoth the Doue-house:'twas no need, I trow,
To bid me trudge.
And since that time it is eleven yeares.

168

Here, the movement runs as fast as the small shadows over the grass. There is but little emphasis, there are but few hard consonants. The words 'Christian', 'beare', 'bitter', 'teachie', 'trow' 'trudge', delay the movement a little, are heavier than the rest of the texture. Otherwise, all is as soft, as feathered, as the breasts of the doves in the house beneath which the old woman sits with the baby Juliet. The running movement is given by the constant use of double-syllabled words arranged in a particular manner throughout the lines, and by putting the single-syllabled words in such places that they are not emphasised, and consequently move more quickly.

Throughout the whole passage the pauses occur, it seems, only for want of breath on the part of the speaker.

I have printed this speech as verse, since it appears in the form of verse in all modern editions. But in the Quartos it is printed as prose, and I think there is much to be said for doing so, since it conveys better the pauseless movement, the quickness, the breathlessness of the old woman's talk. The verse-beat is *not* very strong in this passage. In the debatable sleep-walking speeches in *Macbeth* it *is* very strong,—too strong, in my belief, if it is actually to be spoken as verse, for the situation. This leads me to think that in those speeches of Lady Macbeth, Shakespeare meant the beat to underlie rather than to rule, the sound of the speech,—to be, as it were, a reminder of that Fate-strong will overlaid by sleep, but still, though unconsciously, combating it. But with these exceptions,—still debatable ones—if any speech from Shakespeare *can* be heard as verse, it is probably meant to be spoken thus, no matter in what form it was printed originally. We find, over and over again, prose 'speaking above a mortall mouth'—as in this passage from *As You Like It*,—though this cannot be spoken as verse:

169

Leander, he would haue liued many a fair year, though Hero had turn'd nun, if it had not beene for a hot midsummer night; for, good youth, he went but forth to wash him in the Hellespont, and, being taken with the cramp, was drown'd: and the foolish chroniclers of that age found it was—Hero of Sestos. But these are all lies: men haue died from time to time, and wormes haue eaten them, but not for loue.

It is interesting to compare the speech of Juliet's nurse, already quoted,—its comparative pauselessness, with the false fawning movement of the wicked Queen's speeches in *Cymbeline*,— speeches with a serpentine intertwining motion, where the pauses do not so much stretch or divide the line, as rear themselves up suddenly, like a snake about to strike:

> No, be assur'd you shall not finde me, Daughter,
> After the slander of most Stepmothers
> Euill-eyed unto you: you're my Prisoner, but
> Your gaoler shall deliuer you the keyes
> That locke up your restraint,

and

> While yet the dewe's on ground, gather those floures,
> Make haste; who has the note of them.

In the first passage, the treacherous fawning movement is produced by the trisyllabic words 'stepmother', 'prisoner', 'deliver'.

Nor are these the only passages in these two plays which it may interest us to compare, as regards the effect of texture on the movement.

If, for instance, we examine this fragment of a speech of Mercutio:

... True, I talke of dreames
Which are the children of an idle braine,
Begot of nothing but uaine phantasie;
Which is as thin of substance as the ayre,
And more inconstant than the winde, who wooes
Euen now the frozen bosome of the north,
And, being anger'd, puffes away from thence,
Turning his face to the dewe-dropping south;

we shall see that this air-borne music, whose miraculously-managed pauses,—each like a breath of gentle air—are the result of the varying vowel-lengths, is very different from, is colder than, the lovely and wavering airiness of this speech of Iachimo's:

The Crickets sing, and man's ore-labour'd sense
Repaires it selfe by rest: Our Tarquin thus
Did softly presse the Rushes, ere he waken'd
The Chastitie he wounded. Cytherea,
How brauely thou becom'st thy Bed; fresh Lilly,
And whiter than the Sheetes; That I might touch,
But kisse, one kisse. Rubies unparagon'd,
How deerely they doo it.'Tis her breathing that
Perfumes the Chamber thus: the Flame o' the Taper
Bowes toward her, and would under-peepe her lids,
To see th' enclosed Lights, now Canopied
Under those Windowes, White and Azure—lac'd
With Blew of Heauen's own tinct. But my designe,
To note the Chamber; I will write all downe,
Such, and such pictures. There the window, such
The Adornment of her Bed; the arras, Figures,
Why such and such: and the Contents o' the Story.
Ah, but some naturall Notes about her Body,

Aboue ten thousand meaner moueables
Would testifie, to enrich mine Inuentorie.
O sleepe, thou ape of death, lye chill upon her,
And be her Sense but as a Monument,
Thus in a Chappell lying. Come off, come off;
As slippery as the Gordian knot was hard.
'Tis mine, and this will witnesse outwardly
As strongly as the Conscience docs within,
To the madding of her Lord. On her left Brest
A mole, cinque-spotted: like the Crimson drops
I' the bottome of a Cowslippe. Heere's a Voucher,
Stronger than euer Law could make; this Secret
Will force him thinke I haue pick'd the lock, and ta'en
The treasure of her Honour. No more: to what end.
Why should I write this downe, thats riueted,
Screw'd to my memorie? She hath bin reading late,
The tale of Tereus; heere's the Leefes turn'd downe
Where Philomel gave up. I haue enough,
To the trunk againe, and shut the spring of it.
Swift, swift, you Dragons of the night, that dawning
May bear the Rauen's eye: I lodge in feare
Though this a heauenly Angell, Hell is heere.

                              (Clocke strikes.)

One, two, three; time, time.

    The movement, which is gentle and wavering like the flame of the taper bowing toward Imogen, is the result of the particular arrangement of the one-syllabled, two-syllabled, and three-syllabled words: in several cases the line ends with a three-syllabled word, which gives a flickering sound to the line.

    The texture is of an incredible subtlety. The reasons for this are manifold. Sometimes it is due to the fact that assonantal vowels, placed in close conjunction, are embodied in consonants which have varying thickness or thinness (if we can apply the word 'embodied' or 'thickness' to the unbelievably air-delicate texture of the verse). The *ck* of 'Crickets' in the first line undoubtedly gives the faintest possible body and roundness to the centre of the word, the *Cr* and the *t* the slightest sharpness,—each of an entirely different quality (for the *Cr* stings, while the *t* is sharp, but does not sting). 'Sing' has a slight poignancy, owing to the *ng*, and is therefore longer than its assonance the first syllable of 'Crickets'. There is a tiny sharpening, again, in the second of these faint, dim assonances, 'The Crickets sing'—because 'sing' is a one-syllabled word.

Much of the beauty of the sound is due to the dissonance-assonance scheme that runs through it, and the rhythm, that lovely wavering movement to which I have referred, is, in part, the result of the arrangement of these, the way in which they are placed, sometimes close together (as with the small, dim, then sharpening sound of 'The Crickets sing' and the light *a*'s of 'Perfumes the Chamber thus: the Flame o' the Taper') and sometimes echoing the original sound after a space of some lines. An exquisite effect of dimming and brightening, brightening and dimming, is produced by the use of a vowel, first faint, then brightened, or vice versa,—or by the use of alliterative consonants followed by vowels that are, first bright, then darkened.

Here is an example of the former:

> ... fresh L*i*lly,
> And wh*i*ter than the Sheetes—

and of the latter:

> ... ere he waken'd

173

The Chastitie he wounded.
When, for a moment, the thought of rape enters
Iachimo's mind, with the creeping sound of
                         ... Our Tarquin thus
        Did softly *presse* the Rushes,

there occurs the echo 'fresh Lilly—'fresh' being at once an altered echo of 'presse' and of 'Rushes',—as if these two words were blown together and their changed sound had become a single entity.

And whiter than the Sheetes; That I might touch.

'Touch' is a harder echo of 'rushes'.

        But kisse, one kisse. Rubies unparagon'd,

'kisse' is a distorted dissonantal echo of 'presse'. We may notice, too, the change from the deepened, richened sound of 'Rubies unparagon'd' through the dimmed 'How deerely they doo it.'Tis her' to the brightening

                         ... breathing that
    Perfumes the Chamber thus: the Flame o' the Taper

—this followed by the sound, flickering, bending, and straighten-ing, blowing faintly backwards and forwards like the flame, of

    Bowes toward her, and would under-peepe her lids.

This effect is produced partly by the three dissonantal *o's* that accompany the *w's* of 'bowes', 'toward', 'would', and partly by the fact that, in the two words of double syllables in this line, the first, 'toward', has a second syllable that is accented and fairly long, while the second word, 'under', has a first syllable that is, though accented, very slightly shorter than the 'ward' of 'toward'.

174

*   *   *

One, two, three, time, time,

And almost as Iachimo's dark voice ceases, Time is abolished
and we fall into a dreamless sleep amid the night airs. Then even
the flickering taper, and its little movement that seems as if it
were about to change into a sound, is gone, and we waken to find
that the dark and faintly lightening, exquisite night-music has
flown, and that we are listening to the sound of fluttering wings
wet with dew, to the sound of the music that the clownish Cloten
has brought into Imogen's ante-chamber:

> Hearke, hearke, the Larke at Heauens gate sings,
>   and Phoebus gins arise,
> His Steeds to water at those Springs
>   on chalic'd Flowres that lyes;
> And winking Mary-buds begin
>   to ope their Golden eyes:
> With euery thing that pretty bin,
>   My Lady sweet arise:
>   Arise, arise.

Part of the beauty of that fresh, clear, and soaring movement
comes from the fact of the word 'Hearke' being repeated twice—
(the first time is a kind of springing-board for the second)—
followed by its rhyme 'Larke' in the same line, and also because
there are, for some reason, two little breaths, two little flutters, in
the fourth line, between 'chalic'd' and 'Flowres', and after
'Flowres'. The reason for the first flutter is that the word' chalic'd'
seems drawing itself faintly together, like the calixes of those
flowers when dew splashes down upon them,—(this is caused by

175

the narrow vowels). The reason for the second flutter is that 'Flowres' is a word of one syllable and a fraction. The two flutters, therefore, move in a different direction; the first slightly backward, the second slightly forward.

The whole of the poem is really built upon *in* sounds, sometimes sharp, as with 'sings' or 'winking', sometimes faint, as with 'gins' or 'bin'—these alternating with poignant *i* and *y* sounds ('arise', 'lyes', 'eyes'). It is this, and the particular arrangement of the double-syllabled and single-syllabled words, that give the poem its lovely, incomparably fresh, springing movement.

This is one of the few songs of Shakespeare's that have not been subjected, at one time or another, to wrong printing.

Of the marvellous song from *Measure for Measure* Swinburne, in *Studies of Shakespeare*, wrote: 'Shakespeare's verse, as all the world knows, ends thus:

> But my kisses bring againe,
> > Bring againe,
> Seales of loue, but seal'd in uaine,
> > Seal'd in uaine.

The echo has been dropped by Fletcher, who has thus achieved the remarkable musical feat of turning a nightingale's song into a sparrow's. The mutilation of Philomela by the hands of Tereus are nothing to the mutilation of Shakespeare by the hands of Fletcher.'

Part of the almost unendurable poignance of the marvellous song from *Measure for Measure*: 'Take, oh take those lips away'—I speak of the technical side—is due to the repetition, to the echoes which sound throughout the verse, and part to the way in which the imploring stretching outward of the long vowels in 'Take' and its internal assonance 'againe' (and other words with long high vowels) are succeeded, in nearly every case, in the next stressed foot, by a word which seems drooping hopelessly, as with 'lips', and' forsworne', for instance.

The third line, however:

> And those eyes, the breake of day,

is an exception. Here, all is hope. Indeed, the sound of 'breake' and 'day' rises after the sound of 'eyes'.

A singular beauty, too, is given by the variation in the length and depth of the pauses. Let us examine the song for a moment:

> Take, oh take those lips away,
> that so sweetly were forsworne;
> And those eyes, the breake of day,
> lights that doe mislead the Morne!
> But my kisses bring againe,
> Bring againe,
> Seales of loue, but seal'd in uaine,
> Seal'd in uaine.

Note the lightening dissonance of 'lips' and 'sweetly', the way in which 'breake of day' would echo, exactly, 'take those lips away', but for the fact that 'breake' and 'day' are drawn more closely together by the space of one syllable. Note, too, the beauty of the assonances 'eyes' and 'lights' and how the particular position in which they are placed gives additional poignancy.

To return to the printing of the Songs. There are cases where, to my hearing, it seems that the longer line is right. The causes of speed in poetry are but insufficiently understood by many

177

people. If the following song from *A Midsommer Nights Dreame* is printed thus:

> Ouer hil, ouer dale,
> Thorough bush, thorough briar,
> Ouer parke, ouer pale,
> Thorough flood, thorough fire,

it obviously moves more slowly, because of the pause at the end of each line, than if it is printed thus:

> Ouer hil, ouer dale, thorough bush, thorough briar,
> Ouer parke, ouer pale, thorough flood, thorough fire.

Here, the pause owing to the long vowels is less like a pause than like the stretching of wings. The fairy was evidently in a hurry,— and the flight was even, not a series of hops.

The same applies to certain of the songs of Ophelia,—I think there is much to be said for these being printed so as to give them speed. They are snatches of song, some echoes of old refrains, some outbursts of grief, whirling round and round in that distraught head:

OPHELIA

How should I your true loue know from another one?
By his Cockle hat and staffe and his Sandal shoone.

QUEEN

Alas! sweet lady, what imports this Song?

OPHELIA

Say you? Nay pray you, marke.
He is dead and gone, Lady, he is dead and gone,

At his head a grasse-green Turfe, at his heeles a stone.
O, ho!

QUEEN

Nay, but, Ophelia,—

OPHELIA

Pray you, marke.
White his Shrow'd as the Mountaine Snow.

(*Enter King.*)

QUEEN

Alas! looke heere, my Lord.

OPHELIA

Larded with sweet flowers:
Which bewept to the graue did go,
With true-loue showres.

These are, sometimes, swift as the spring rain,—sometimes sounding like the wind. But in the last song of Ophelia's, however, the unbearably poignant

And will he not come againe,

there is a complete breakdown of the heart. The springs are broken, the slow grief has pierced through madness, dispelled even the impetus that madness gives:

And will he not come againe?
And will he not come againe?
No, no, he is dead;
Go to thy Death-bed,

179

He neuer will come againe.

His Beard was as white as Snow,

All Flaxen was his Pole:

He is gone, he is gone,

And we cast away mone:

God ha' mercy on his Soule.

Incidentally, a light is thrown on the sentence

Well, God'ild you. They say the Owle was a Bakers Daughter. Lord, wee know what we are, but know not what we may be. God be at your Table!

by the fact that a person was arrested in the time of Mary I for the libel of writing that King Philip preferred 'Bakers' daughters' to Queen Mary. From this we may gather that 'Bakers' daughters' was a synonym, in that age, for women of loose character.

If this be so, the phrase has more than one meaning: The daughter of joy, the light liver, becomes the harbinger of death and of woe. This is one meaning.

But I have wandered far from the Fairy's Song of the *Midsommer Nights Dreame*, and must return to it.

Ouer hil, ouer dale, thorough bush, thorough briar,

Ouer parke, ouer pale, thorough flood, thorough fire,

I do wander euery where, swifter than the Moone's sphere;

And I serue the Fairie Queene,

To dew the orbs upon the green;

The Cowslippes tall her pensioners bee,

In their gold coats spots you see:

Those be Rubies, Fairie fauors,

In those freckles liue their sauors.

180

I must go seeke some dew drops heere,
And hange a pearle in euery cowslippe's eare.

In the line

The Cowslippes tall her pensioners bee,

the three-syllabled word 'pensioners' has a little trembling sound,
like that of dew being shaken from a flower.

Note, too, the effect on the rhythm of the rising, brightening
dissonances and the darkening dissonances and, too, of the allit-
eration in the first two lines,—also the still sharper and brighter,
flying effect, brought about by the internal rhymes 'dale' and
'pale', put at exactly the same place within the lines:

Ouer hil, ouer dale, thorough bush, thorough briar,
Ouer parke, ouer pale, thorough flood, thorough fire;

'hil' brightens into 'dale',' bush' deepens into 'briar', then dark-
ens into 'parke', this rises again and brightens into 'pale', so
that we see the fairy flying through the sunlight and shadow of
that immortal spring. Again in the line

In their gold coats spots you see,

after the bright assonances of 'gold coats', we have a slightly
darker dissonance to 'coats' in 'spots'.

A fresh and lovely balance is given to the lines

These be Rubies, Fairie fauors,
In those freckles liue their sauors,

by the fact that though 'Rubies' and 'freckles' appear to be equiv-
alent in length, actually they are not so. 'Rubies' is longer, because
of the vowel-sound.

Elsewhere in the *Midsommer Nights Dreame*, what miracles are performed by the use of sharpening *r*'s, as in the first two lines of

> … hoary-headed frosts
> Fall in the fresh lap of the crimson Rose,
> And on old Hyem's thinne and Icie crowne
> An odorous Chaplet of sweet Sommer buds
> Is, as in mockery, set.

Though here the beauty of the sound is due as much to the deep breath of the alliterative *h*'s (hoary-headed) and the dimming. *f*'s which succeed these; and, too, to the wonderful design of *o*'s.

But the texture of the whole scene is one endless miracle.

An enchanted beauty is given by the lingering *l*'s in 'Lady' and 'Land' of Tytania's

> Then I must be thy Lady; but I know
> When thou hast stolne away from Fairy Land

—a sound echoed again in 'loue' and 'Phillida' in the succeeding lines:

> And in the shape of Corin sate all day,
> Playing on pipes of Corne, and uersing loue
> To amorous Phillida.

There is a strange darkening and concentration, changing of shape, from 'Corin' to the sound of 'Corne'.

1. On Elisions in Shakespeare

As I have pointed out elsewhere, elisions in blank verse are

182

often but *pretended* elisions, and are an excuse for variety, since the supposedly elided syllables exist and are not muted. Sometimes, as in *King Lear*, these pretended elisions produce the effect of the shaking of a huge and smoky volcano—(we find this effect, too, though it is less vast, over and over again in *Paradise Lost*)—or they swell the line, moving it slightly forward, rearing it upward, like the beginning of a tidal wave, and presaging the final break and the shattering roar of that wave. Sometimes, again, as in Perdita's speech, pretended elisions give a line the faintest possible increased length, or produce a faint dip in the line (the word 'Flowres', for instance, has this last-mentioned effect):

> ... O Proserpina!
> For the Flowres now that frighted thou let'st fall
> From Dysses Waggon! Daffadils,
> That come before the Swallow dares, and take
> The windes of March with beauty; Uiolets dim,
> But sweeter than the lids of Juno's eyes,
> Or Cytherea's breath; pale Prime-Roses,
> That dye unmarried, ere they can behold
> Bright Phoebus in his strength, a Maladie
> Most incident to Maids; bold Oxlips, and
> The Crowne Imperiall, Lillies of all kinds,
> The Fleure-de-Luce being one. O, these I lacke
> To make you Garlands of, and my sweet friend,
> To strewe him o're, and o're.

If we examine this, we shall find that the beauty of the sound owes much to the fluctuations caused by the pretendedly elided syllables in 'Flowres' and 'Uiolets', and to Shakespeare's genius in the use of the falling foot,—(Proserpina,

Cytherea,—names which fall with a flowerlike softness and sweetness). Then, again, much beauty is given by the fact that the last syllable of 'Daffadils' echoes the vowel-sound of 'Dysses', and that 'lids' is an echo (but the faintest possible fraction higher) of 'dim'. Note the change in the texture when we come to:

> ... pale Prime-Roses,
> That dye unmarried, ere they can behold
> Bright Phoebus in his strength.

Here all is brighter, owing to the high echoing *i* sounds following the dim *i* of 'lids'. Nor is this the result of association alone, for in the rest of the fragment the texture varies, growing richer with the sound of 'bold' and 'Crowne' in the phrase

> ... bold Oxlips, and
> The Crowne Imperiall.

One of the most wonderful of all examples of Shakespeare's genius in the use of the Falling Foot is in Desdemona's line:

> Sing all a greene Willough must be my Garland.

I was once privileged to hear this miraculous line changed to

> Sing all a greene Willough my Garland must be!!

2. A Note on Sonnet XIX

This is, in all probability, the greatest sonnet in the English language, with its tremendous first lines:

184

Deuouring Time, blunt thou the Lyons pawes,
And make the earth deuoure her owne sweet brood;
Plucke the keene teeth from the fierce Tygers yawes,
And burne the long liu'd Phoenix in her blood;
Make glad and sorry seasons as thou fleets,
And do what ere thou wilt, swift-footed Time,
To the wide world and all her fading sweets;
But I forbid thee one most hainous crime,
O, carue not with thy howers my loues faire brow,
Nor draw noe lines there with thine antique pen,
Him in thy course untainted doe allow
For beauties pattern to succeeding men.
    Yet doe thy worst, ould Time; dispight thy wrong,
    My loue shall in my uerse euer liue young.

The huge, fiery, and majestic double vowels contained in 'deu-ouring' and 'Lyons' (those in 'Lyons' rear themselves up and then bring down their splendid and terrible weight)—these make the line stretch onward and outward until it is overwhelmed, as it were, by the dust of death, by darkness, with the muffling sounds, first of 'blunt', than of the far thicker, more muffling sound of 'pawes'.

This gigantic system of stretching double vowels, long single vowels muffled by the earth, continues through the first three lines:

    And make the earth deuoure her owne sweet brood;
    Plucke the keene teeth from the fierce Tygers yawes,
    And burne the long-liu'd Phoenix in her blood.

The thick p of 'pawes' muffles us with the dust, the dark hollow sound of 'yawes' covers us with the eternal night.

The music is made more vast still by the fact that, in the third line, two long stretching double vowels are placed close together ('keene teeth'), and that in the fourth there are two alliterative *b*'s,—'burne' and 'blood', these giving an added majesty, a gigantic balance.

Epilogue

Two Poems by Edith Sitwell

(I) A Mother to her Dead Child

The winter, the animal sleep of the earth is over
And in the warmth of the affirming sun
All beings, beasts, men, planets, waters, move
Freed from the imprisoning frost, acclaim their love
That is the light of the sun.
                                So the first spring began
Within the heart before the Fall of Man.

The earth puts forth its sprays, the heart its warmth,
And your hands push back the dark that is your nurse,
Feel for my heart as in the days before your birth.
O Sun of my life, return to the waiting earth
Of your mother's breast, the heart, the empty arms.
Come soon, for the time is passing, and when I am old
The night of my body will be too thick and cold

For the sun of your growing heart. Return from your new
    mother
The earth: she is too old for your little body,
Too old for the small tendernesses, the kissings
In the soft tendrils of your hair. The earth is so old
She can only think of darkness and sleep, forgetting
That children are restless like the small spring shadows.
But the huge pangs of winter and the pain
Of the spring's birth, the endless centuries of rain
Will not lay bare your trusting smile, your tress,
Or lay your heart bare to my heart again
In your small earthly dress.
And when I wait for you upon the summer roads
They bear all things and men, business and pleasure, sorrow
And lovers' meetings, mourning shades, the poor man's
    leisure,
And the foolish rose that cares not ever for the far tomorrow.
But the roads are too busy for the sound of your feet,
And the lost men, the rejected of life, who tend the wounds
That life has made as if they were a new sunrise, whose human
    speech is dying
From want, to the rusted voice of the tiger, turn not their
    heads lest I hear your child-voice crying
In that hoarse tiger-voice; 'I am hungry! am cold!'
Lest I see your smile upon lips that were made for the kiss that
    exists not,
The food that deserts them,—those lips never warm with love,
    but from the world's fever,
Whose smile is a gap into darkness, the breaking apart
Of the long-impending earthquake that waits in the heart.
That smile rends the soul with the sign of its destitution,

188

It drips from the last long pangs of the heart, self-devouring,
And tearing the seer.

      Yet one will return to the lost men,
Whose heart is the Sun of Reason, dispelling the shadow
That was born with no eyes to shed tears,—bringing peace to
 the lust
And pruriency of the Ape, from the human heart's sublimity
And tenderness teaching the dust that it is holy,
And to those who are hungry, are naked and cold as the worm,
 who are bare as the spirit
In that last night when the rich and the poor are alone,
Bringing love like the daily bread, like the light at morning.
And knowing this, I would give you again, my day's darling,
My little child who preferred the bright apple to gold,
And who lies with the shining world on his innocent eyes,
Though night-long I feel your tears, bright as the rose
In its sorrowful leaves, on my lips, and feel your hands
Touching my cheek, and wondering 'Are those your tears?'
O grief, that your heart should know the tears that seem empty
 years
And the worlds that are falling!

(II) Green Song

To David Horner

After the long and portentous eclipse of the patient sun
The sudden spring began
With the bird-sounds of Doom in the egg, and Fate in the bud
 that is flushed with the world's fever—

189

But those bird-songs have trivial voices and sound not like
    thunder,
And the sound when the bud bursts is no more the sound of
    the worlds that are breaking.—
But the youth of the world, the lovers, said, 'It is Spring!
And we who were black with the winter's shade, and old,
See the emeralds are awake upon the branches
And grasses, bird-blood leaps within our veins
And is changed to emeralds like the sap in the grasses.
The beast-philosopher hiding in the orchards
Who had grown silent from the world's long cold
Will tell us the secret of how spring began
In the young world before the Fall of Man.
For you are the young spring earth
And I, O Love, your dark and lowering heaven.'

But an envious ghost in the spring world
Sang to them a shrunken song
Of the world's right and wrong—
Whispered to them through the leaves, 'I wear
The world's cold for a coat of mail
Over my body bare—
I have no heart to shield my bone
But with the world's cold am alone—
And soon your heart, too, will be gone—
My day's darling.'

The naked Knight in the coat of mail
Shrieked like a bird that flies through the leaves—
The dark bird proud as the Prince of the Air,
'I am the world's last love. ... Beware—
Young girl, you press your lips to lips

That are already cold—
For even the bright earthly dress
Shall prove, at last, unfaithfulness.

His country's love will steal his heart—
To you it will turn cold
When foreign earth lies on the breast
Where your young heart was wont to rest
Like leaves upon young leaves, when warm was the green spray
And warm was the heart of youth, my day's darling.

And if that ghost return to you—
(The dead disguised as a living man)
Then I will come like Poverty
And wear your face, and give your kiss,
And shrink the world, and that sun the heart
Down to a penny's span.

For there is a sound you heard in youth
A flower whose light is lost—
There is a faith and a delight—
They lie at last beneath my frost
When I am come like Time that all men, faiths, loves, suns
    defeat
My frost despoils the day's young darling.

For the young heart like the spring wind grows cold
And the dust, the shining racer, is overtaking
The laughing young people who are running like fillies
The golden ladies and the ragpickers
And the foolish companions of spring, the wild wood lilies.'

But the youth of the world said, 'Give me your golden hand

That is but earth, yet it holds the lands of heaven
And you are the sound of the growth of spring in the heart's
     deep core,
The hawthorn-blossoming boughs of the stars and the young
     orchards' emerald lore.'

And hearing that, the poor ghost fled like the winter rain—
Sank into greenish dust like the fallen moon
Or the sweet green dust of the lime-flowers that will be
blossoming soon—And spring grew warm again.—

No more the accusing light, revealing the rankness of Nature—
All motives and desires and lack of desire
In the human heart, but loving all life, it comes to bless
Immortal things in their poor earthly dress—
The blind of life beneath the frost of their great winter
And those for whom the winter breaks in flower
And summer grows from a long-shadowed kiss.
And Love is the vernal equinox in the veins
When the sun crosses the marrow and pith of the heart
Among the veridian smells, the green rejoicing.
All names, sounds, faiths, delights and duties lost[1]
Return to the hearts of men, those households of high heaven.
And voices speak in the woods as from a nest
Of leaves—they sing of rest,
And love, and toil, the rhythms of their lives,
Singing how winter's dark was overcome,

---

[1] Dorothy Wordsworth, in the *Grasmere Journal*, May 8, 1802, wrote 'I wept
for names, sounds, faiths, delights and duties lost', from a poem on Cowley's
wish to retire to the Plantations.

And making plans for tomorrow as though yesterday
Had never been, nor the lonely ghost's old sorrow.
And Time seemed but the beat of heart to heart,
And Death the pain of earth turning to spring again
When lovers meet after the winter rain.
And when we are gone, they will see in the great mornings
Born of our lives, some memory of us, the golden stalk
Of the young long-petalled flower of the sun in the pale air
Among the dew. ... Are we not all of the same substance,
Men, planets, and earth, born from the heart of darkness
Returning to darkness, the consoling mother,
For the short winter sleep—O my calyx of the flower of the
    world, you the spirit
Moving upon the waters, the light on the breast of the dove.

THE END

193

A NOTE ON THE AUTHOR

Edith Sitwell was born in 1887 into an aristocratic family and, along with her brothers, Osbert and Sacheverell, had a significant impact on the artistic life of the 20s. She encountered the work of the French symbolists, Rimbaud in particular, early in her writing life and became a champion of the modernist movement, editing six editions of the controversial magazine Wheels. She remained a crusading force against philistinism and conservatism throughout her life and her legacy lies as much in her unstinting support of other artists as it does in her own poetry. Sitwell died in 1964.

Made in the USA
Middletown, DE
11 November 2024

64346931R00115